A BRIEF HISTORY OF BIDDEFORD

A BRIEF HISTORY OF
BIDDEFORD

EMMA R. BOUTHILLETTE

Prologue by Mayor Alan Casavant
Epilogue by Delilah Poupore

THE History PRESS

Published by The History Press
Charleston, SC
www.historypress.net

Front cover, top: McArthur Public Library; *bottom*: Benjamin Williamson Photography.
Back cover, top: McArthur Public Library; *bottom*: McArthur Public Library.

First published 2017

Manufactured in the United States

ISBN 9781467136143

Library of Congress Control Number: 2017931801

For the droves of French Canadians who arrived in Biddeford, Maine, searching for jobs in the textile mills, but especially for my great-grandparents who were part of that movement and my grandparents and parents who passed down to me many Franco-American traditions.

Contents

Prologue

I grew up during a thriving era for Biddeford. In the 1950s and 1960s, the city was the hub of York County and an economic engine. Many of my ancestors were French Canadians who arrived in the early part of the twentieth century to work in the brick industrial fortresses that lined Main Street. They were machinists, spinners, dyers and weavers. They worked long hours in the loud, humid mills to provide for their large families. At home, and even still in school, most of them spoke French.

I spent part of one summer, as my grandparents did, working in those very same mills. I worked third shift tending the cards—huge machines that pummeled the fibers into workable thread. The noise was deafening. The heat and humidity were unbearable. The belts and gears turning the machines whistled and hummed all night long, and production never stopped. My co-workers were good, hardworking people who were, in many ways, the backbone of the city. Many of them had worked for the mill for more than twenty years. They were survivors in a world of monotony and repetition, and their ability to survive in that environment created a work ethic unmatched in the state of Maine.

The textile industry, and particularly the mill owners, dominated the physical and economic landscape of Biddeford since the industry arrived in the mid-nineteenth century. The work defined the many generations who grew up while the mills still flourished. However, my generation and generations to come were often warned about the tedious, grinding work inside those brick walls. My father pushed me to study for good grades and to go to college. He and my mother did not want me working in the mill. Many of my friends' parents uttered the same warnings and urgings. In some ways, the mills started to carry a negative connotation, despite paying wages that allowed many residents to achieve middle-class status. Many teenagers wanted to escape the shadow that the mills cast on Biddeford. They wanted go to college and find job security; many were willing to move away to do so.

I heeded my parents' warning, yet the mystique of the mill's history intrigued me. The vastness of the mill complex and the architecture of the buildings attracted me. It is often overlooked that Pepperell Manufacturing Company was once a world-renowned producer of textiles. The company dominated Biddeford's economy for more than a century before production was moved south. In the 1980s, a national recession hit Biddeford in full force, reducing the number of textile jobs and decimating downtown. Stores shut their doors, unable to compete with large-scale grocery chains and box retail stores that moved into Maine. City officials approved the construction of a trash incinerator alongside the mills, which further eroded the city's Main Street and perpetuated despair. People familiar with Biddeford in its glory years believed that the city was doomed and would never regain its former prominence in southern Maine.

However, by the turn of the twenty-first century, the prophesy of catastrophe proved false. Individuals "from away" began to move to the community, including those who could not afford the skyrocketing costs of rents in Portland and individuals from all over New England and places farther west. All saw a promise of possibilities in the downtrodden city. They saw potential in the landscape, the architecture and the residents themselves. Their optimism, energy and innovation sparked the birth of a new, creative economy. Monthly art walks enticed people to stroll Main Street and the mill spaces that had been redeveloped. City Theater, designed by famous Maine architect John Calvin Stevens in 1895, underwent a significant renovation and raised the bar for its productions. The arts emerged as a central focus of this renaissance, and Main Street began to waken from its long slumber.

The beautiful geography that drew Richard Vines to the area has continued to be instrumental in the economic vitality of the city. Adaptation to changing times has long defined Biddeford's people—from the first winter when Vines and his men survived the harsh weather, to the battles of the French and Indian Wars, to the evolution of Biddeford's economy

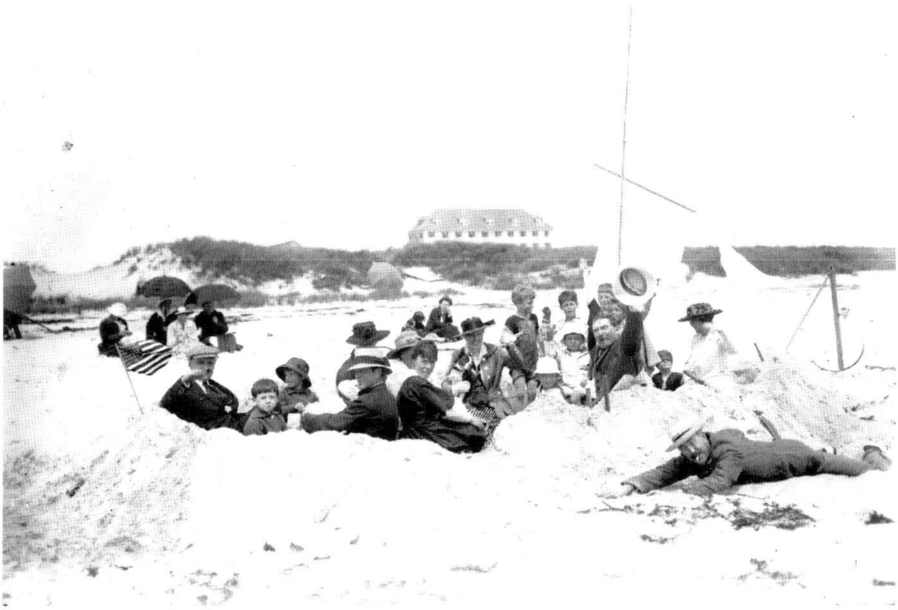

Beachgoers create a "boat of sand" at Biddeford Pool, circa 1916. *McArthur Public Library Archive.*

from fishing and lumbering to textiles. In the wake of the recent economic recession, residents and newcomers have continued to adapt and thrive. Biddeford has made national news with its redevelopment of the old mills, the addition of unique restaurants, the increased support for the arts and the resurgence of shops downtown. Most important, a new pride is emerging in this coastal community.

Biddeford today is welcoming many middle-class families who are looking for affordable living with the amenities of city life. Younger generations of Biddeford residents are returning to their hometown. Entrepreneurs from Boston and Brooklyn, finding the economy approachable, are moving here to live and work. People are embracing the beauty of our rocky coast and beaches and enjoying the proximity it offers to larger cities like Portland, as well as easy access to Maine's gorgeous mountains.

Prior to becoming Biddeford's mayor, I taught social studies at Biddeford High School. I have always believed a community's history is integral to its identity. The residents, the economy and the culture of the past have left an indelible imprint on the present. We continue to revere our heritage while growing as a community and evolving with the times. When you consider Biddeford's past alongside its present, the whole is worth more than the sum of its parts.

Alan Casavant, a lifelong Biddeford resident, is serving his third term as the city's mayor. He retired in 2011 as a teacher of psychology, American history and global studies at Biddeford High School.

Acknowledgements

This book would not exist today if not for my University of New England classmate Camille Smalley. She prompted me to tackle this project head on and provided much-needed encouragement along the way. Of course, I cannot thank Camille without also thanking our mutual mentor and college professor Elizabeth A. DeWolfe, who unsuspectingly introduced Camille and me to each other through her coursework and inspired our passion for history.

To special collections guru Renée DesRoberts and her fellow staff at McArthur Public Library, I give immense thanks. The last time I spent so much time at McArthur Library, I was probably eight and was repeatedly told I could only take out three books at a time when I precariously carried a stack of twelve to the front desk. To the staff, thank you for letting me borrow far more than three books during the course of my research. To Renee in particular, you are a rock star. Thank you for assisting me with imagery for the book and always knowing just what I should read when I was seeking the most specific bit of information. Readers, if anything in the following pages leaves you wanting more, go to the library; the staff will help you in your pursuit of knowledge. It is impossible for me to calculate the value McArthur Public Library brings to Biddeford's downtown.

To my parents, Diane and Peter Bouthillette, I can never say "thank you" enough. You have seen me through some challenging times, to say the least. I do not think I would have survived without you. You only questioned me a little when I came bounding through the door one evening to tell you I had declared my major at the University of New England and would spend the following three years studying English literature. When my career path after college hit a lot of potholes on its rather winding way, thank you for never doubting my ability to succeed even when I doubted myself. I love you both to the moon and back.

I would be remiss to not thank all my French Canadian ancestors as well. From the ones who decided to uproot the family and come work in Biddeford, to my grandparents—Gisele and Roland Bouthillette and Lionel and Madeleine Croteau—who stayed in this richly historical city, thank you. Thank you for the beach days, the cribbage lessons, the endless skeins of yarn you wasted teaching me how to knit and, most of all, for your fascinating stories.

To Alan Casavant and Delilah Poupore, who generously agreed to write the prologue and epilogue to this book before I even drafted a chapter, thank you. As a senior at Biddeford High School, I had the pleasure of taking global studies dual taught by Jim McCann and Mayor Casavant. I denied loving history back then, but I realize now that global studies sparked my interest in projects I would later pursue in life. I met Delilah when I was still

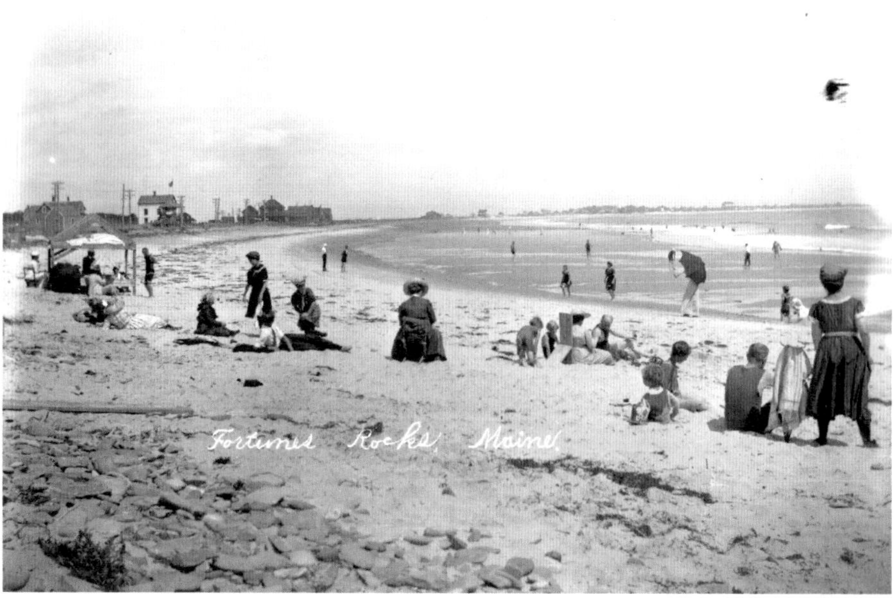

Biddeford's three miles of sandy beach has long drawn visitors for recreation, including these local sunbathers, circa 1917. *Robert H. Gay Photograph Collection, courtesy of McArthur Public Library.*

a reporter and she was new to Heart of Biddeford. We would later attend the National Main Street Conference in Detroit together and reaffirm that Biddeford is and is still becoming an awesome place, thanks to the countless hours of hardworking, forward-thinking individuals.

Thank you to two talented modern photographers, Benjamin Williamson and Kari Wehrs. The moment I saw Benjamin's images on Facebook, I prayed he would allow me to include his work in the book. He is the talent behind the modern image on the cover. The moment I met Kari in August 2007, I knew we would not only be collaborators during our semester at Salt Institute for Documentary Studies but also be collaborators on life. She is the talent who created the tintype and digital rendering of my author photo.

A final thank-you goes out to Biddeford's visionaries—the dreamers and doers. Thank you for seeing the potential and acting on it, creating the rich, vibrant history this city has to offer.

Part I

Colonial Times

1
The First Winter

Dawn awakens Maine's coastline. The sun crests the horizon beyond East Point Sanctuary and illuminates Biddeford's three miles of sandy beach. This hour is peaceful. Lobster boats circle traps offshore, collecting their catch. The thrum of motors and the caw of gulls can be heard ever so slightly over the crashing waves. Soon, summer vacationers and locals will flood the beach, building sandcastles, surfing waves or lazing in the sun. Biddeford's coastal community is a popular destination for tourists with rental properties lining the beach and harbor. However, many visitors, and even some residents, may not know that this land has drawn the interest of visitors for more than four hundred years.

Biddeford is positioned on the southern coast of Maine, along the western bank of the Saco River as it spills into the Atlantic Ocean. The Sokoki (often referred to by European explorers as Saco), members of the regional Abenaki tribe, inhabited the bay long before the area was discovered. In 1603, Martin Pring and Robert Salterne were among the first explorers to note Biddeford's coastline as a point of interest in their travels. Pring wrote in his travel log, "The perilous voyage across the Atlantic [in the *Speedwell*] was made in safety."[1] The crew of thirty men first arrived in the New World in a bay area, known today as Maine's midcoast region, where the Penobscot River meets the ocean. Their mission was to establish a trade industry with the "ignorant savages" rumored to be living along the coast.[2] Finding none, the crew moved on, following the rocky coastline south to another harbor, the area we know today as Saco Bay. Pring found this area, with its protected

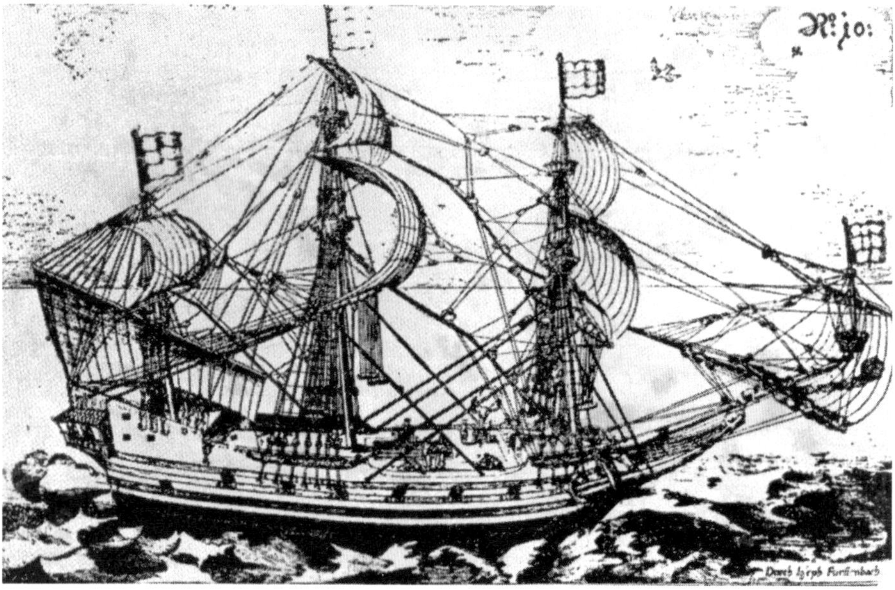

A hand-drawn rendering of what Captain Richard Vines's vessel may have looked like when he returned to Winter Harbor in 1630. *McArthur Public Library Archive.*

coast and sandy beaches, more favorable than the rocky coast farther north, but he failed to meet the natives despite finding extinguished fire pits and abandoned campsites.[3] A second trip to the area is documented in Pring's travel log, in which he writes:

> *This river is named the Shawakotoc, and is half a mile broad; it runneth into the land fiftie dais journey, but foure daies from the entrance it is so narrow, that the trees growing on each side doe so crosse with their boughs and bodies on the other as it is permitted not by any means to passé with boates that way....At the end of this River, there is a lake of foure daies journey long and two daies broad, wherein are two Ilands.*[4]

It is believed Pring learned this information from the Sokoki living near the bay.

Two years later, French cartographer Samuel de Champlain anchored in the same bay of which Pring made note. He wrote in his travel log, "a large number of Indians came toward us upon the bank of the river and began to dance...these people showed they were much pleased" to see Champlain's interest in the region.[5] He described the Sokoki people he met as fit and active. They wore feathers and furs, with black and red paint smeared on their faces. A rudimentarily sketched map found in Champlain's journal documents the geography of the bay and coastline. Demarcations indicate a long stretch of sandy beach, areas of marshland and vast fields, wooded forests and a couple of islands in the bay. Among the geographical indicators, Champlain drew a fort and cabins where people native to the land had settled. While Pring's account only noted evidence of settlements, Champlain's experience is the first known documentation of interaction with people native to the New World.[6]

The explorers who encountered the land where the Shawakotoc River (which colonists later renamed the Saco River for ease of pronunciation) met the sea agreed on one fact—they deemed the area favorable for settlement. Champlain's conclusion was that, "the climate here [in Saco Bay] is more temperate and better...than at other places on this coast."[7] These early impressions of the New World supported European interests in colonizing new land.

These explorer reports piqued the interest of Sir Ferdinando Gorges, an English aristocrat. Gorges, born of a prosperous, landowning family and an active member of the royal military, decided to invest his moderate wealth in further expeditions with the hope of settling small villages in the New World. The first crew under Gorges's direction left England in June 1607 in two ships, *Gift of God* and *Mary and John*, under the command of Captain George Popham and Raleigh Gilbert, respectively, with about 120 people.[8] They anchored near the mouth of the Kennebec River and set out to build a fort and storehouse near modern-day Bath and Brunswick. By December, 45 of the settlers had left, and "when Captain Richard Davies arrived from England in the spring of 1608, he found the men had endured a severe winter and were discontented."[9] The remaining men returned to England, abandoning the settlement.

Despite this failure, Gorges remained hopeful that settlement was viable. It was not until 1616 that Gorges was able to recruit a captain and crew for a second attempt. He hired Captain Richard Vines and a crew of thirty-two men, offering extra wages to sweeten the mission. He directed Vines slightly farther south than where Gilbert had anchored. The mission was to weather one full year in the sheltered bay that Champlain had mapped a little more than a decade earlier, confident this area would result in a successful settlement.[10]

When Vines and his crew arrived, they dropped anchor near the area known today as Biddeford's Back Bay. The protected harbor offered an

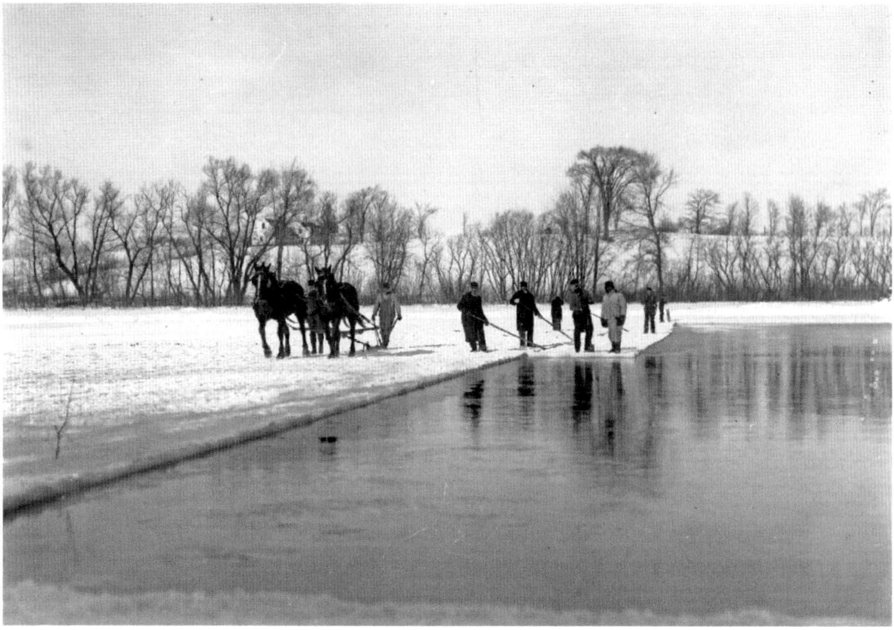

A horse-drawn cutter is scoring the ice along the Saco River as men break it away in big floes, circa 1912. *McArthur Public Library Archive.*

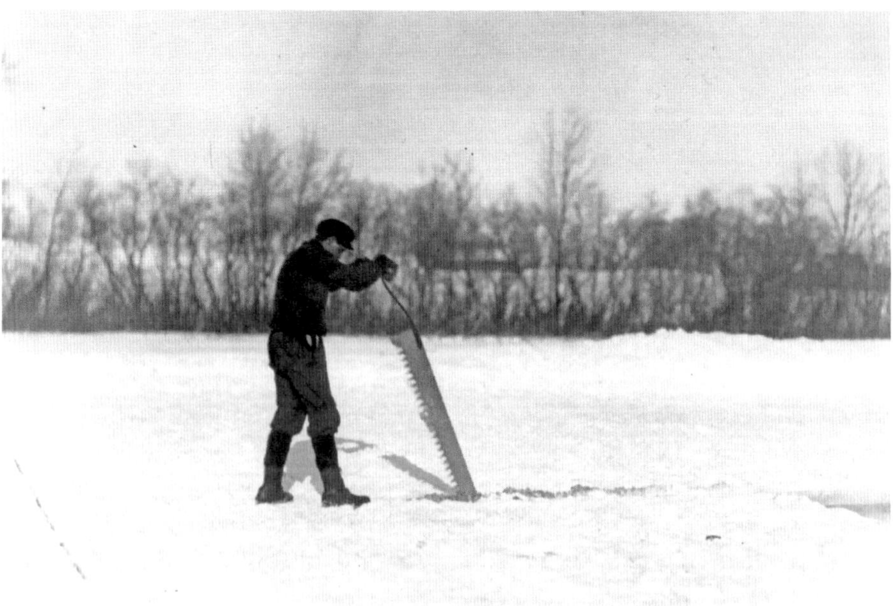

Ice was cut from the Saco River and then sold to residents. *McArthur Public Library Archive.*

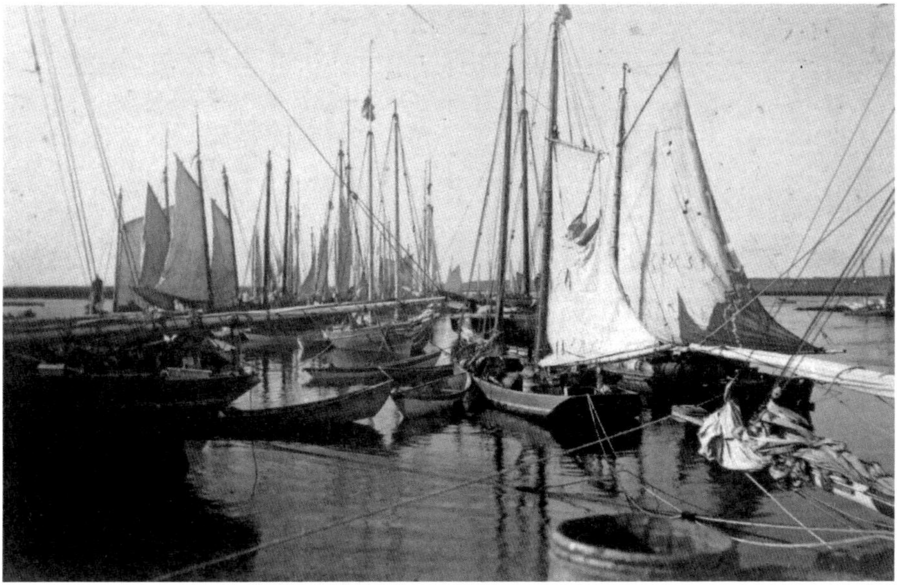

Herring was a primary catch for Biddeford Pool's fishing industry. A fleet of fishing vessels is pictured around 1890. *McArthur Public Library Archive.*

ideal location to leave the ship and go ashore. In the area occupied today by multimillion-dollar homes, Vines ordered his crew to set up camp. The Sokoki who inhabited the area soon arrived to greet the newcomers. The number of native people was fewer than Vines expected, but they welcomed him and the crew to the region.[11]

Over the course of that first winter, the Sokoki became a valuable resource to the explorers. They showed Vines and his men wild plants safe to harvest, crops viable for growing and game to hunt and fish along the coastline. The Sokoki diet included hearty vegetables such as corn, beans and squash; wild game such as venison, rabbit and fowl; and a variety of fish, including salmon, sturgeon and herring.[12] Vines and his men learned from the Sokokis' way of life, not only in terms of food, but also shelter. They replicated the Sokoki wigwams, building crude domed cabins essential to survival in the first winter.

During his stay, Vines took the opportunity to explore the coastal area and inland regions. From the mouth of the river, which became known as the Saco River, Vines followed the snaking waterway northwest about 136 miles to its source. At the end of his first year in the New World, Vines and his crew returned to England. He reported back to Gorges, providing a full

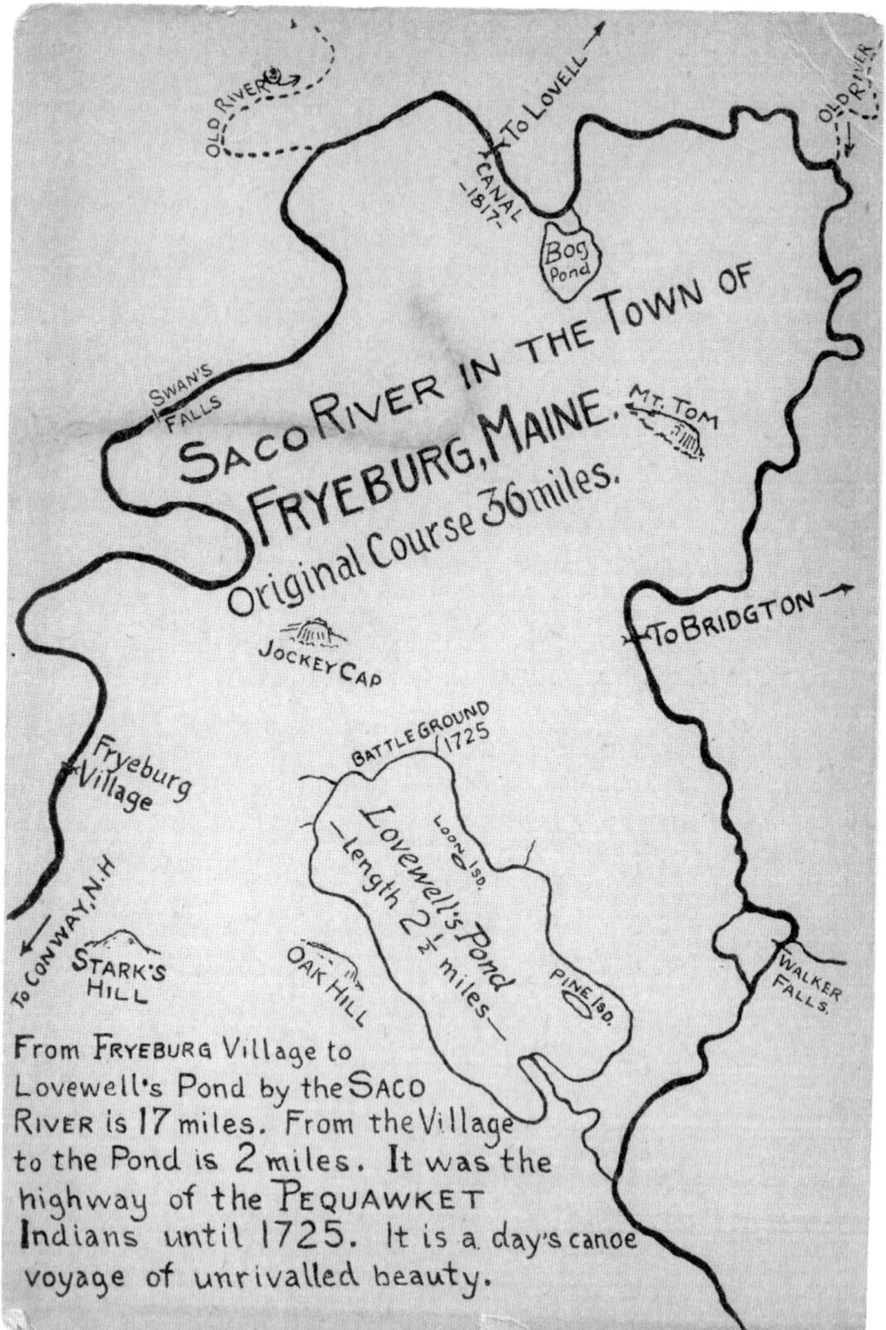

A not-to-scale sketch of the Saco River, which stretches from Fryeburg, Maine, to Biddeford and Saco. *Richard N. Carr Collection, courtesy of McArthur Public Library.*

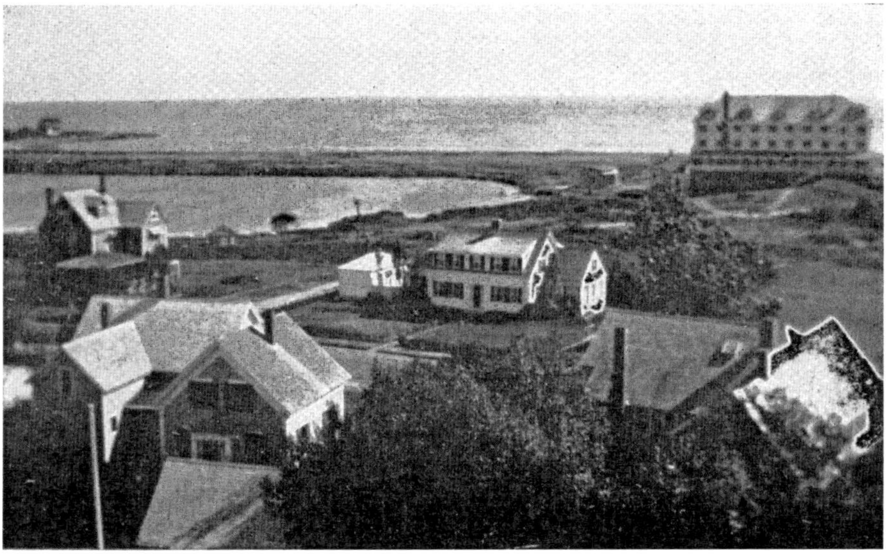

An aerial view of Biddeford Pool, circa 1920. *Richard N. Carr Collection, courtesy of McArthur Public Library.*

description of the land he explored, the people he met and his assessment of where they settled—aptly dubbed Winter Harbor. Vines believed the coastal area was hospitable and would support a settlement.[13]

2

A Village Named Saco

The first year in Winter Harbor is widely considered the founding of Biddeford, Maine. However, a formal European settlement of the Saco Bay region would not occur for another thirteen years, and little is known about the intrepid Vines between 1617 and his return to Winter Harbor in 1630. During this gap in Biddeford's history, the area became a frequent stop for explorers and fishermen. Christopher Levett, a captain of the Royal Navy, spent five nights in the bay during an explorative voyage. In his journal, he wrote of the poor conditions, "the wind being contrary and the weather very unseasonable, having much rain and snow and fog."[14] Levett's crew was forced to spend a few nights in Winter Harbor, where they erected their own wigwams to take shelter. During the short stint, he noted that the area was favorable, taking comfort in the fact that "we had fowl enough for killing, wood enough for felling and good, fresh water enough for drinking."[15] Levett's journals, which were later published in England, further proved the area's viability for colonization.

By 1622, two years after the *Mayflower* dropped anchor and the Pilgrims settled Plymouth, Massachusetts, Sir Ferdinando Gorges secured a grant to the "Province of Maine." With this grant, Gorges gave a patent to Levett to settle modern-day Portland and a patent to Vines to return to Winter Harbor. The twenty-thousand-acre property officially granted to Vines by the "Lords of the Council for the affairs of New England" on February 22, 1630, included four miles of oceanfront and eight miles inland along the western bank of the Saco River—approximately the same boundary of

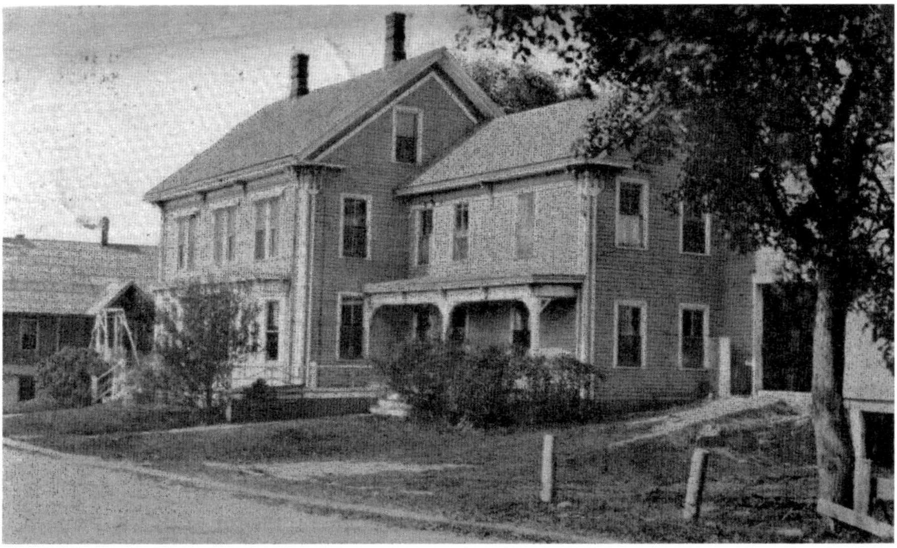

Winter Harbor Inn, Biddeford Pool, circa 1938. *Richard N. Carr Collection, courtesy of McArthur Public Library.*

Biddeford's city limits as drawn today. Vines paid an annual rent of twelve pence per one hundred acres, approximately twenty-five dollars a month by today's standards, and committed to bring fifty settlers to the area.[16]

Vines began his journey back to Winter Harbor with Englanders willing to immigrate and establish a new life in the New World. The group returned to Winter Harbor and settled in an area known today as Biddeford Pool. Around the same time, a patent was granted to Captain Richard Boynthon and Thomas Lewis to establish a village on the eastern bank of the river.[17] The settlers on either side of the river likely spent their first year in wigwam structures similar to those Vines built during his first year in Winter Harbor. Soon, the colonists began felling trees to build permanent frame houses reminiscent of their English dwellings, making the New World feel more like home.

The following year, herd animals, including hogs, sheep, goats and cows, were imported from England to the New World. It would be several years before horses were introduced to the colonies.[18] During these early years, settlers continued to learn from the Sokoki. The native people taught the colonists what crops were best to grow and what food was best to harvest, hunt or fish. The settlers' diets were similar to those of the Sokoki, including wild game and hardy plants, in addition to the meat from imported herd

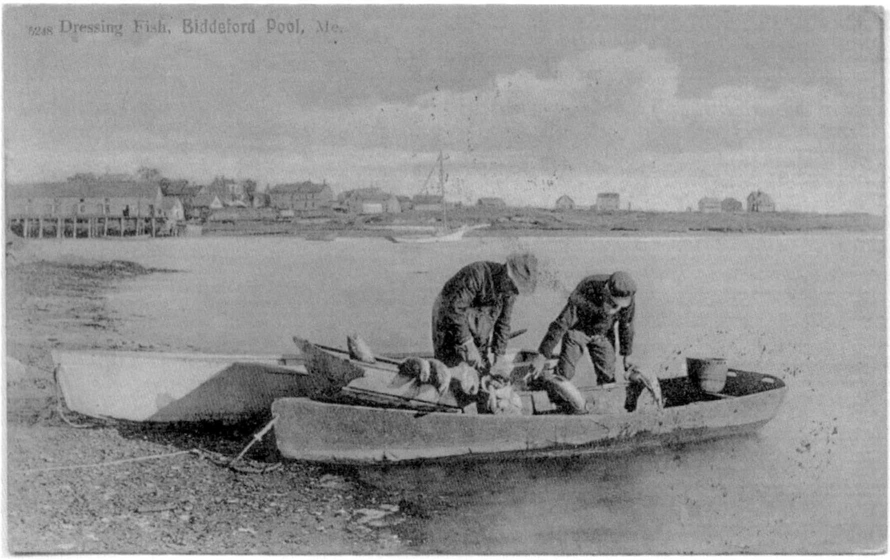

Fishermen fillet their catch on the shore at Biddeford Pool, circa 1906. *McArthur Public Library Archive.*

animals. This lifestyle required the early English settlers to be nothing less than productive. These first members of the English colonies were "men of hardy mould [*sic*]; vigorous, energetic and well able to turn their hands to anything that gave promise of yielding a respectable livelihood."[19] Compared to their lives in England, "this was a rude, primitive life, but it produced a sturdy race of people."[20] Though primitive, the settlers were diversified in their skills, becoming adept at many trades in the community.

Gorges was pleased. The settlement's success lured more immigrants across the Atlantic Ocean. As new families arrived, the population grew and the settlement expanded inland along the riverbank. Homes were built as far inland as the river's rapid waterfalls, about five miles away from the village of Winter Harbor. They populated areas known today as Camp Ellis, Hills Beach and Biddeford Pool, expanding into the areas of modern-day downtown Biddeford and Saco. Even these early settlers differentiated themselves by the small pockets where they lived and whether their home lay to the east or west of the river.

"Each year added new numbers to the little groups of settlers, until Saco Bay became an important point in the new world."[21] Settlers acquired one-hundred-acre tracts of land, for which they paid Vines five shillings a year for the term of the land lease. For those of lesser wealth, deed terms included

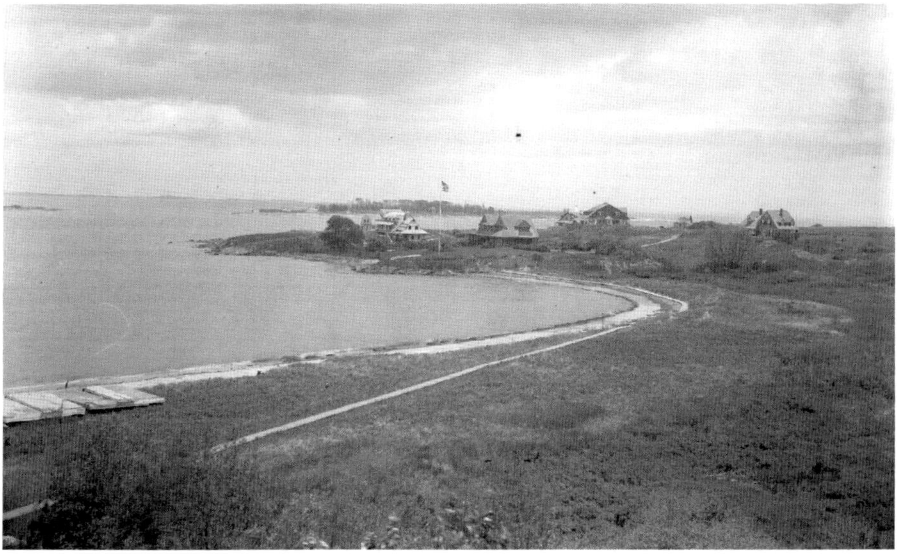

Wood Island can be seen in the distance overlooking East Point in Biddeford Pool, circa 1910. The island became home to the thirteenth lighthouse in the United States when it was built in 1808. *Robert H. Gay Photograph Collection, courtesy of McArthur Public Library.*

stipulations to provide food for feasts or labor for harvest season.[22] Property lines were drawn, and settlers used granite boulders to erect low-lying rock walls as boundaries. Some of these walls still snake through the woods today.

By the last quarter of the eighteenth century, the area on both sides of the river was dubbed Saco—a name derived from Sokoki. Families managed large herds of livestock, fields were producing abundant harvests and Winter Harbor had become a bustling fishing community. Fishermen made their catches in the river, bay and deep waters of the Atlantic Ocean. They used one of the many islands offshore—including Wood, Negro, Stage, Basket and Ram—as a staging facility to dry and salt their catches before selling them in their village, Portland and Boston. Fish, including cod, hake, haddock and pollock, were caught in abundance. These fish could fetch anywhere from two dollars to four dollars per one hundred pounds. In the early years of America, fifteen dollars a year was considered a sufficient wage for a family, leading historians like Daniel Owen to believe the people of Saco lived comfortably during the seventeenth century.[23]

Gorges lived for seventeen years after the successful settlement of Winter Harbor. From the time he began investing his wealth in colonization, until his death, Gorges never actually stepped foot in America. He spent his life's

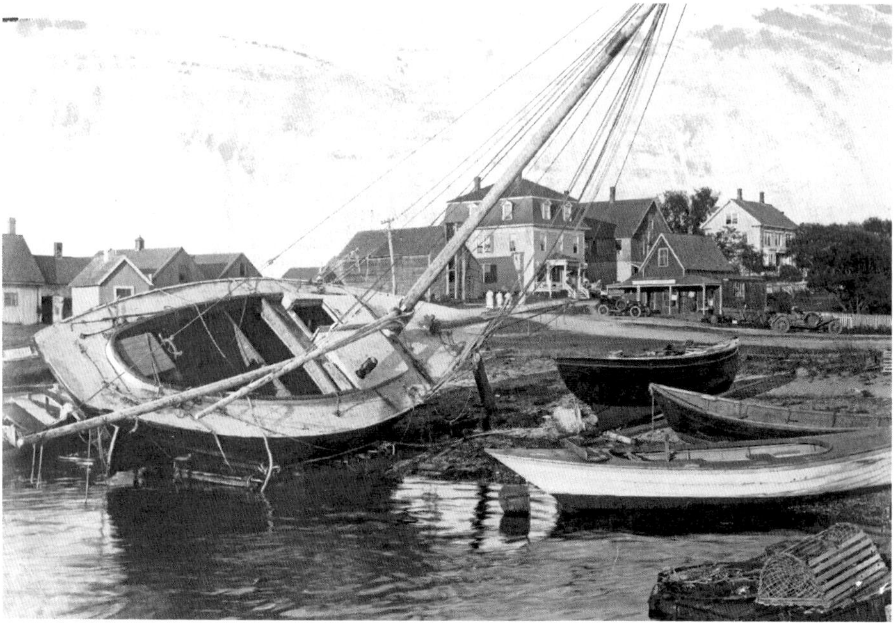

The docks of Biddeford Pool, circa 1910. *McArthur Public Library Archive.*

fortune entirely on his endeavor to establish settlements in Maine, and he died poor. However, he considered his work in colonizing these villages a huge success in expanding English rule.

By the time of his death, Saco was thriving. The settlers had developed a decent working relationship with the Sokoki tribesmen and lived mostly in peace. It was said "the worst enemies in the first days [of colonization] were not the red men, but the lawless whites, some of whom infested the coast as pirates."[24] However, the settlers' fortitude would be challenged as the turn of the century neared. There was conflict among settlers regarding the way government should be established and with the local tribes, who felt threatened by the increasing presence of white men.

3

Developing Colonial Government

With the coming of more settlers and growing villages throughout Maine, Massachusetts and south along the Eastern Seaboard, the need for a form of government was becoming more pressing. With that need came conflict between two distinctly different schools of thought.

The settlers of Maine were mostly of the mindset that life should be governed as it was in England. Rather than waste their time debating theology, "the settlers of Saco...were hard working fishermen and farmers, bent on earning their bread honestly."[25] When they immigrated to America, those who settled in Maine brought with them what they knew of government and religion, which led to a mix of views, including those of Puritanism (strict moral rules), Anglicanism (faith in communion with the episcopal Church of England) and Antinomianism (moral law is of no use—all that is needed is faith). A Puritan minister, Thomas Jenner, called the people he met in Maine "very superstitious," not necessarily abiding to the formalities in worshipping God—mostly following Anglican traditions—unlike the people of Massachusetts Bay, who stuck with a more rigid Puritan form of religion.[26]

With staunch Puritan beliefs came a vastly different way of governing those who settled in Massachusetts. They took the laws of England and created stricter governance. Colonists were mandated to attend church on Sundays and practice a Puritan lifestyle. By nature, it didn't take long for the lackadaisical ways adopted in Maine to create tension with those of fellow settlers about one hundred miles to the south.[27]

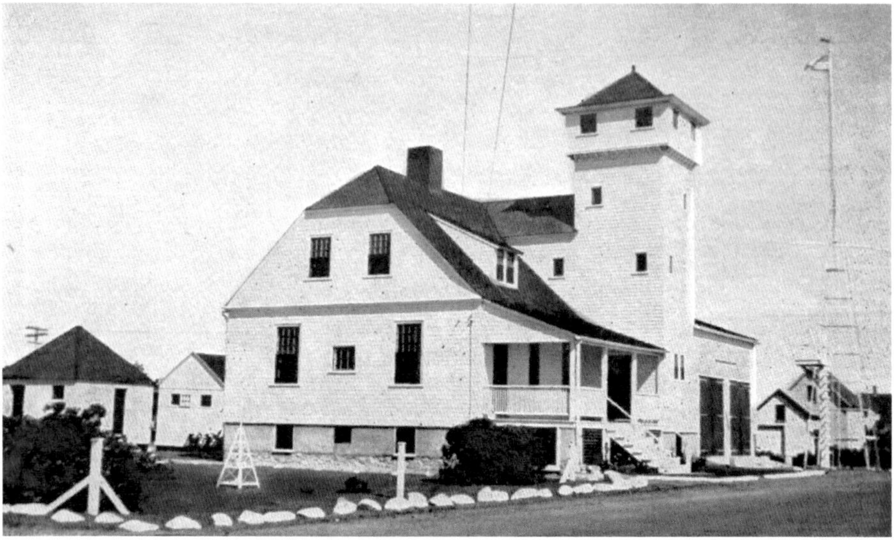

The Coast Guard Station was situated on the outer curve of Biddeford Pool with an expansive view of the ocean and was active in many rescues. The building has now been converted to a private residence. *McArthur Public Library Archive.*

In addition to dispatching explorers to develop settlements in the New World, Ferdinando Gorges took it upon himself to assist with the establishment of a more formal government. In 1636, he dispatched his nephew William Gorges to oversee the creation and execution of laws. William Gorges arrived in time to oversee the first general court, which was held in the Saco home of a well-respected captain, Richard Boynthon, on March 25, 1636.[28] The court agreed, following English law, that "no offense was so insignificant as to be considered beneath the attention of the learned justices."[29] This led to the persecution of minor disputes and transgressions, including debts, drunkenness, swearing, slander and working on the Sabbath Day.[30] The first general court fined four people five shillings apiece for intoxication, fined two others for card playing and rash speech and summoned one man for idleness and not providing for his family.[31] This newly established court not only enforced the laws of England, but it also assumed legislative duties, creating new laws, deciding on issues of criminal and civil matters and overseeing the inventories of estates, wills and acts of administration.[32]

Officials of the Plymouth Council in Massachusetts were determined to overthrow the administration Gorges was trying to establish. With his nephew serving as his eyes and ears, Gorges added Vines as his steward general, representing "Gorges in a special way, being that gentleman's agent in transfers of land and responsible to him in large measures for the everyday supervision of the province."[33] When William Gorges had to return to England, Gorges dispatched his other nephew Thomas Gorges to continue having an English representative in Maine's general court.

Thomas Gorges arrived and was immediately faced with opposition. The people of Maine had become fearful of the risk that they would be locked into servitude under an authoritarian government. But Thomas Gorges "assured the settlers they would be governed by [no] act but with their [own] consent."[34] With the help of well-respected settlers, Thomas Gorges and Vines enacted a rudimentary, albeit effective governing structure that offered economic viability and a code of morals to live by. This structure allowed settlers to have a more formal governing body while also being mindful of the community's resources. Thomas Gorges had the foresight to limit the number of trees being felled, the livestock roaming on open fields and the fish caught from the sea. Fearing the settlers would wipe the area clean of natural resources, he attempted to stymie that in any way possible. While Thomas Gorges did well to have this sure-footed government in place prior to returning to England, it would not be strong enough to abate the Plymouth Council.[35]

Members of the Plymouth Council governing Massachusetts were critical of the government forming in Maine. The council tried to edge its way into Maine with the creation of the "Plough Patent," which issued grants to land that had already been claimed by settlers in Saco and other Maine villages. However, those who purchased a patent became disappointed with the land granted, abandoning what they purchased. The Plough Patents had all but been forgotten when George Cleeves solicited the assistance of British lawyer Alexander Rigby to bargain a purchase of the "Plough Patent."[36]

On Thomas Gorges's departure from Maine, Cleeves arrived with the patent in hand with a plan to overtake the colony. This was the second attack Cleeves had made on Vines's character and property, and he hoped this new "crusade against the officers of Sir Ferdinando Gorges and all others who adhered to the original proprietors' cause" would be more successful than the previous.[37] Cleeves slanderously attacked Vines. Despite Vines's continued support by settlers, it was not enough to defeat Cleeves's conniving plan. After two years of fighting for his patent, Vines surrendered, sold his remaining property in Saco and moved to Barbados. His departure left Saco and Maine incredibly vulnerable not only to Cleeves but also to the Plymouth Council.

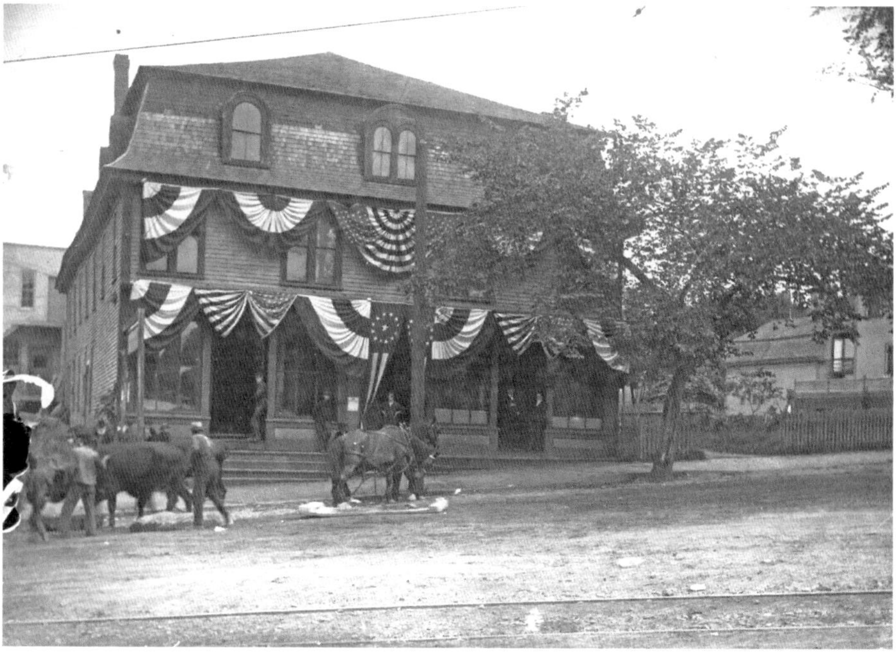

Draft horses and oxen haul granite by the Nickel Theater—decorated for the city's fiftieth anniversary celebration—for the foundation of the Journal Building on September 16, 1905. *McArthur Public Library Archive.*

The settlements in Maine were vulnerable when Gorges died. The Massachusetts governing body was quick to usurp control of the colony to its north and ordered all Maine residents to abide by Plymouth Council law with a formal act dated July 5, 1653. However, "the submission of the inhabitants [of Maine] was not, by any means, unanimous."[38] Many tried to rebel, including the heir of Sir Ferdinando Gorges who came out of the woodwork to stake his claim on the settlements his father funded. The young Ferdinando Gorges saw King Charles II's rise to the throne as an opportunity to inherit Maine and take it under his control. The king honored the young man's inheritance, and Ferdinando Gorges traveled to the land his father never stepped foot on. After such an ardent fight to obtain his inheritance, Sir Ferdinando Gorges's son sold the colony back to Massachusetts in 1678 for a sum of £1,250, ending a brief period of independence for Maine.[39]

Maine remained a district of Massachusetts until its secession on March 15, 1820, when Maine became the country's twenty-third state. The assimilation of Maine under the Plymouth Council was not well received, often leading to conflict among colonists. This conflict, in addition to the competition between England and France over the conquest of new land, only increased the strained relations between settlers and the native tribes who were being pushed away from their easternmost territories. Minor disagreements turned into small battles, ending the peaceful cohabitation and igniting the first of many conflicts now referred to as the French and Indian Wars.

4

The End of Peaceful Cohabitation

Early in the arrival of Europeans to the New World, native tribes were welcoming and helpful. A working relationship was established in which settlers learned from the regional tribes, and the native people traded harvest, catch and crafts for more sophisticated tools and fineries introduced by colonists. However, as the population of settlers grew exponentially and plots of land were claimed, the relationship strained. All along, "despite the temptations of the traders' blankets and pots and tools, the Abnakis [*sic*] never surrendered their pride and became dependent servants."[40] Rather, the Sokoki's fellow Abenaki and other tribes tried to hold on to their own culture, traditions and beliefs. At times, "they seemed to possess sufficient skills as politicians and diplomats to play the French-English rivalry for their own ends, profiting independently from the era of international trade."[41]

As conflict between the English and French progressed, tribes in the northeastern region of the New World found greater opportunity in leveraging the European warring for their benefit. Frustrated with settlers claiming ownership to land viewed by native people as theirs, King Philip, chief of the Wampanoag of Narragansett Bay, was among the first to break the peace and attack settlers near Providence Plantation. On June 24, 1675, tribesmen plundered the trading house of Mr. Thomas Purchase, kidnapped settlers and burned down homes. There was bloodshed on both sides. Word of this conflict quickly spread, inspiring other tribes to plan attacks on settlers. Likewise, the English colonies prepared for the first wars to be fought in the New World.[42]

This era of conflict between Saco settlers and the Sokoki has inspired folklore, stories that have endured centuries. One story claims that Sokoki would slaughter a cow among the villagers' herd and use its bell to lure in farmers and then slaughter them, too. Another story is that of the "Curse of the Saco River." Many books of history and various websites recount the story of some drunk British sailors who decided to test the well-perpetuated myth that "savage babies" were born able to swim like animals. It is said these sailors flipped the canoe of a woman, tossing her and her baby into the chilly waters of the Saco River. The mother and child were able to escape the water, but the baby later died. In this story, it so happens the baby was that of Squando, the supposed chief of the Sokoki, and this cruel act was the final straw in peaceful relations between the local tribe and settlers of Saco. As the folklore goes, Squando cursed the river in his fury; three men were destined to die on the Saco River annually. The curse would only lift once all white men were gone. While the far-fetched story cannot be qualified, deaths on the river prompt retelling of the local story each year.[43]

The curse may simply be folklore, but the same cannot be said for the series of conflicts and strife that occurred during the French and Indian Wars. The Wampanoag and Androscoggin tribes had launched attacks on settlers throughout the Northeast long before the Sokoki and their fellow Abenaki joined in. By the time the Sokoki planned their first onslaught, settlers in Saco learned of bloodshed elsewhere. Ultimately, it was a friendly member of the Sokoki who prompted residents to prepare.[44]

Major Phillips gathered fellow villagers in his garrison on the western bank of the Saco River. On the morning of September 18, 1675, they awoke to find smoke billowing across the river as Captain John Boynthon's home was burned to the ground. Finding no one on the eastern bank, the Sokoki crossed the river, and the men in the garrison braced for battle.[45]

In addition to setting blaze to homes, the Sokoki targeted lumber mills near the river's waterfall, hoping the white men would evacuate the garrison and attempt to save their livelihoods. When the settlers did not leave the garrison, the Sokoki continued their siege and surrounded the building. As the Sokoki neared, the men in the garrison took to arms and began firing on the tribesmen. This first attack in Saco lasted a full day before the Sokoki retreated, providing a brief relief. Major Phillips departed his garrison and followed the footpaths along the river to Winter Harbor. He warned the residents, "houses were all destroyed, and many of the people slain." King Philip's War had "burst upon them in sudden fury" and spurred the French and Indian Wars, which continued into the eighteenth century.[46]

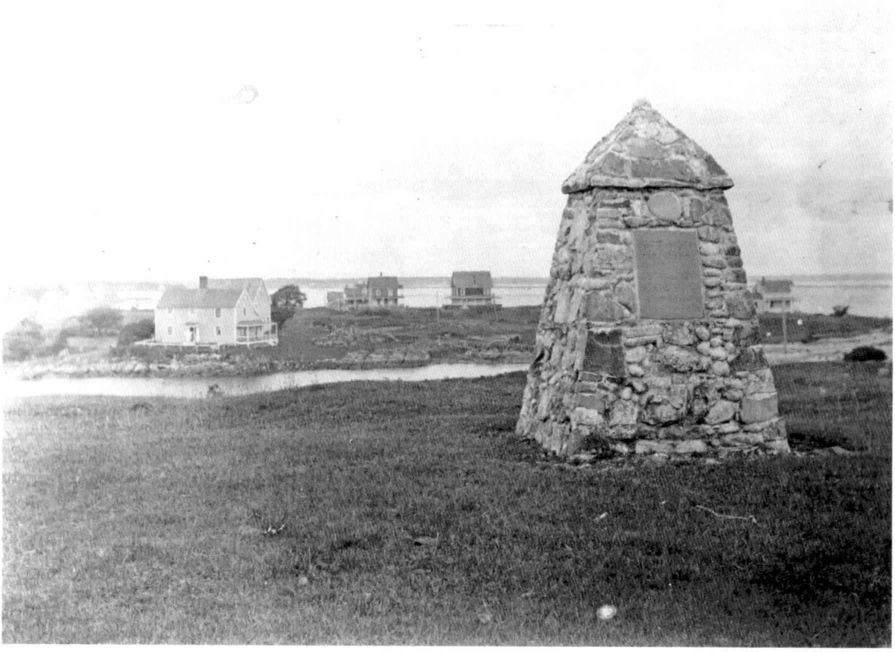

A monument marking Fort Mary in Hills Beach, circa 1911. *Robert H. Gay Photograph Collection, courtesy of McArthur Public Library.*

Conflicts were followed by peace, only to be disrupted again with surprise attacks on the settlers. While Saco experienced the warring firsthand, the town was mostly spared from excessive depredation during King William's War (1689–97). Unlike the story of Squando's baby, other incidents in the area are documented, and they depict just how uncertain life was during the wars. Captain Humphrey Scamman's son left their home to deliver a mug of beer to his father tending the field. En route, he spotted Sokoki approaching, and the boy retreated to alert his mother. Unfortunately, it was too late—the Scamman family was trapped in their home. The Sokoki demanded to see Captain Scamman, so Mrs. Scamman led the men to her husband, but only after receiving assurances from the Sokoki that her family would be kept safe. The tribe promised their safety and took the whole family captive, fleeing to French-occupied Canada. Despite the harrowing event, the tribe kept their word, and the Scammans eventually returned to Saco unharmed, only to find a full mug of beer still sitting on the dresser just inside the door where the boy had placed it on reentering their home. The mug itself remains preserved at the Saco Museum as a part of history.[47]

Saco town records are all but nonexistent during the decades in which the French and Indian Wars raged on. Governance became secondary to survival, and the population dwindled as "many inhabitants had been driven away by the constant deadly fear of Indian savagery [and] that those who remained were either too upset or too few to even hold a town meeting."[48] It took multiple attempts to create peace once again in the New World, but "the Kennebecs, Sokokis, and Penobscots, never eager for the war, were among the first to accept and help work out the [Peace of Casco] treaty's terms."[49] This treaty called for the release of all refugees to their rightful homes and retribution paid by the settlers to the local tribes. "To the Abnakis [*sic*], the imposed peace seemed better than war, but still lacking in that essential ingredient, mutual understanding; lacking, too, in any political system that would allow for continuing discussions of the issues between the societies."[50]

Over time, the population of Sokoki and other tribes who formerly inhabited the region known today as New England were pushed west and north, with most finding refuge in French Canada. "Finally, with Maine calmed down, it appeared that lives and living could be put back together," and the population rebounded.[51] With peace also came a petition for change. Captain Scamman sought to rename the area of Saco after the township from where most of the settlers came—Bideford, Devonshire, England. With approval from Massachusetts governance, the area known for nearly seventy years as Saco—encompassing land to the east and west of the river—was renamed Biddeford.[52]

5

A Settlement's Rebirth

As Biddeford's population steadily grew in the wake of the French and Indian Wars, the first quarter of the eighteenth century became a critical turning point for the coastal colonial village. A century after Vines's first winter along the Saco River, a well-known merchant—Sir William Pepperell—arrived and became the town's first major investor.

Pepperell, born on June 27, 1696, grew up during the French and Indian Wars. Education at the time was rudimentary at best, but Pepperell's parents hired a tutor to teach him navigation and surveying. This "constant activity in the open air, voyages on the sea and exploration in the Maine woods [allowed Pepperell to have] many an encounter with hostile Indians [that] developed in him a superb physical strength and endurance," and offered him a competitive edge over his peers.[53]

Pepperell's business savvy led him to develop the largest mercantile firm in the colonies during the mid-eighteenth century. By the time he was twenty-one, Pepperell was captain of a company infantry; he was quickly promoted to major lieutenant colonel. At the age of thirty, he was appointed as Kittery's representative in the Massachusetts legislature and a member of the Massachusetts Council. He later served as chief justice, a position he held until the time of his death on July 6, 1759.[54]

Pepperell "saw the untold possibilities of [Biddeford]" and invested in the area through a large purchase of land, which included two-thirds of Captain Bonython's original patent as well as land on the western riverbank.[55] On this property, he erected a sawmill near the rapid falls of

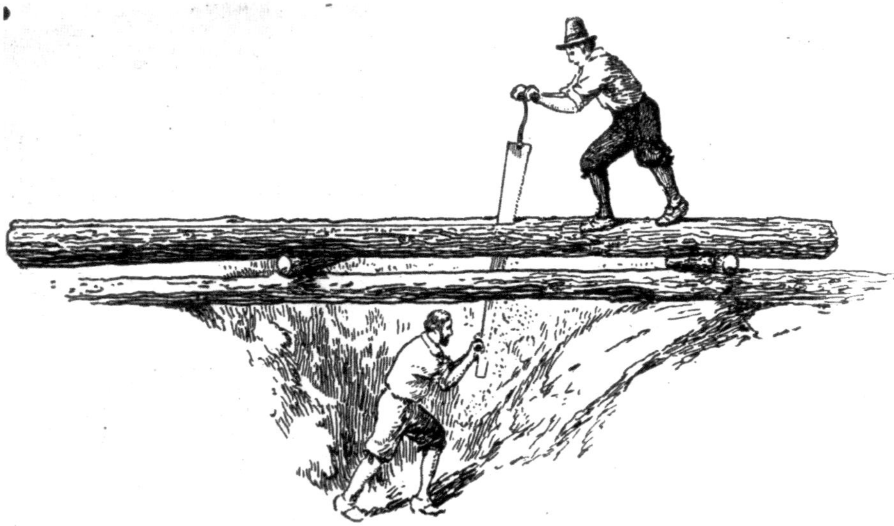

Log Sawing in 1630

An illustration of the act of log sawing as it would have been done when Biddeford was first settled in 1630. *McArthur Public Library Archive.*

the river, built a home for himself and parsed out lots of land in private sales and donations.[56]

While Vines is credited as the founder of Winter Harbor, the initial settlement in the area we know now as Biddeford, Pepperell's legacy is equally important to the area's history. He would be canonized as a man of "infinite caution, sound judgment, strong resolution and due regard to detail" and respected by his successors as the founding father of Biddeford's commerce.[57]

During Pepperell's most influential years, business in Biddeford began to flourish, and the town became more developed. Early colonists spent a significant amount of time fishing, farming and living off the bounty of the land. However, this lifestyle would sustain the community for only so long, and new endeavors began populating what would soon become a downtown. Early entrepreneurs utilized their craftsmanship to make a living as cabinet makers, tanners, cobblers, furniture builders, hat makers and so forth. Whatever path these villagers chose, it was hard work and they found themselves "struggling to make a living, all in building the foundation for a community in which their children and grandchildren would live for generations."[58]

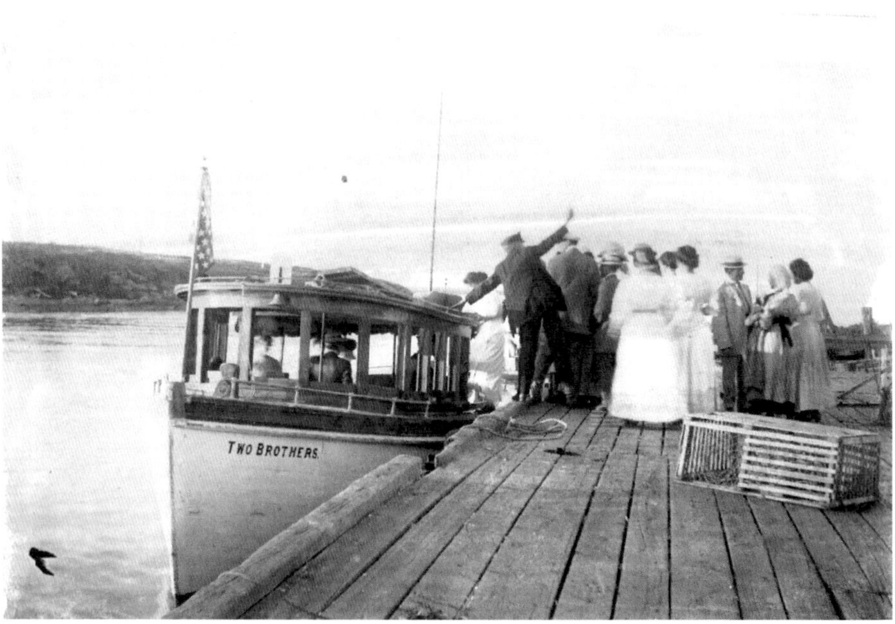

A vessel named *Two Brothers* launches from a dock in Biddeford Pool, circa 1910. *McArthur Public Library Archive.*

With the increase in the area's trade and commerce, residents found they could no longer rely on the worn footpaths between Winter Harbor and the village forming by the falls. While the river remained integral to travel, roadways were becoming increasingly necessary and, indeed, a requirement. As an English colony under the rule of the Plymouth Council of Massachusetts, all of its residents from Wells to Falmouth were ordered "to build roads 'sufficient for horse and man' between towns."[59] Action on this order was significantly delayed by the ongoing conflicts of the French and Indian Wars, but peacetime renewed the sense of urgency to build passable roadways. Often working from the footpaths they already used, residents "cut down trees, grubbed out stumps and rocks, laid logs over runs and brooks." The roads they built were "wide enough for riders on horseback or for an ox-team."[60] The major routes connecting towns were known as King's Highways, the first of which to run through Biddeford came around 1730.

Residents also resurrected a ferry service that ran regularly through the day, allowing people to easily cross Saco Bay from Winter Harbor to the area we know as Camp Ellis. A second ferry was added to cross the river closer to the falls. Despite the ferry service, crossing the river during the harsh winter months remained a treacherous and often arduous task. It did not take

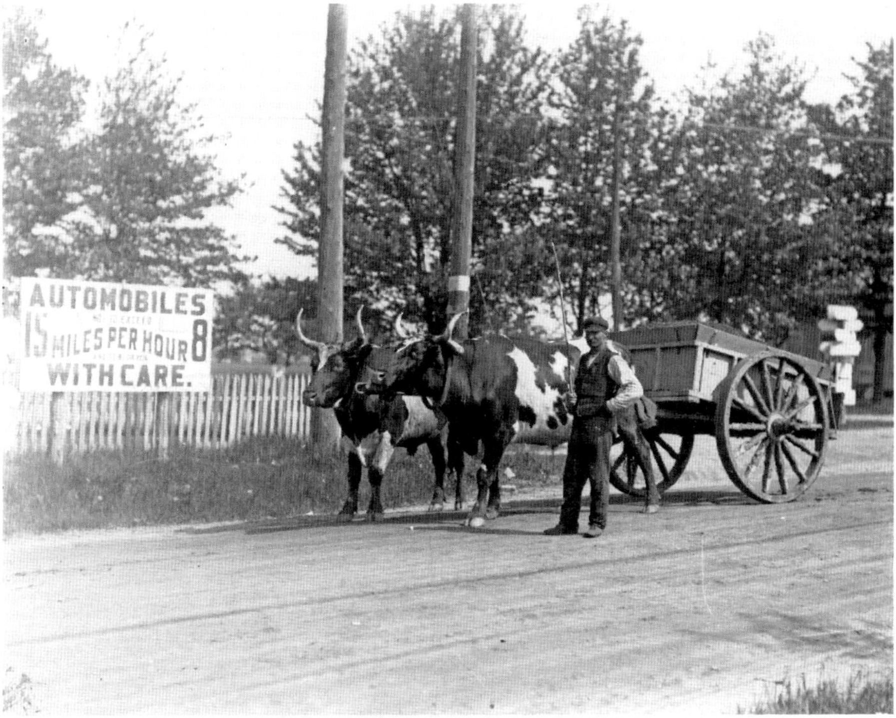

Circa 1910, an ox team belonging to Robert Gilpatrick at the "Five Points" intersection, where a speed limit sign indicated eight miles per hour maximum if heading toward town and fifteen miles per hour maximum if heading toward Arundel. The same intersection today is dominated by two sets of four-way traffic lights. *Robert H. Gay Photograph Collection, courtesy of McArthur Public Library.*

residents long to recognize that a bridge spanning the river at its narrowest points by the falls would greatly ease travel between the villages. Pepperell won a lottery that was established to fund the raising of a bridge. This first bridge over the Saco River opened in 1760. The project cost the residents £1,200, an estimated $200,000 today. A second bridge situated upstream was built seven years later by Biddeford's second prominent landowner and apprentice to Pepperell, Colonel Thomas Cutts.[61] While the new roadways and bridges made land travel a whole lot easier than it had been during the early days of settlement, the Saco River and travel by ship still remained integral to Biddeford's economic success.

By this time, the area's lumber industry was already a century old, having started out of necessity to build homes and business infrastructure. Lumbering remained Biddeford's primary industry through the late 1700s.

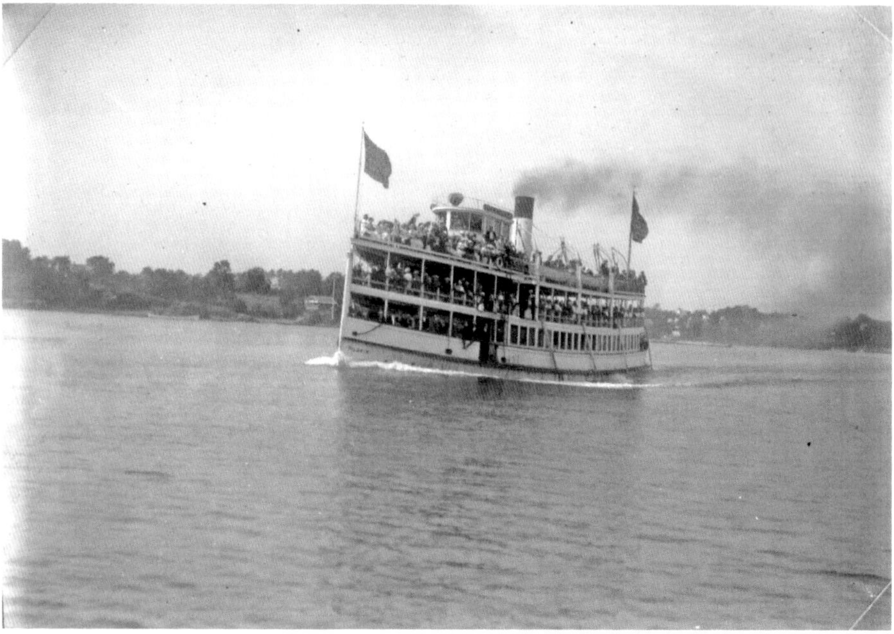

A steamer on excursion sailing upstream on the Saco River, circa 1912. *Charles E. Moody Photograph Collection, courtesy of McArthur Public Library.*

> *Not only did the British mast trade center in the Saco River Valley, but domestic housing and coastal demands required vast quantities of lumber. By 1772, the hustling river men were driving logs from as far away as Fryeburg. Mills went up wherever an enterprising citizen could put a wheel.*[62]

In fact, Biddeford's industry "contributed heavily to the formation of American logging techniques and folklore, and Maine woodworkers pioneered the industry as it moved westward across the United States."[63] By the end of the eighteenth century, there were seventeen sawmills clustered around the Saco River falls, approximately five miles inland from the Atlantic Ocean. The large felled trees that floated down the river to mills were processed into timber beams, shingles, clapboards and staves, among other products. At one point, production was so high that a thick layer of sawdust coated the river. Ever the resourceful Yankees, locals repurposed the accumulating sawdust to insulate large blocks of ice used for preserving perishable foods. Processed wood was then shipped from Saco Bay south to major colonial hubs and east to England.[64] This industry, which required

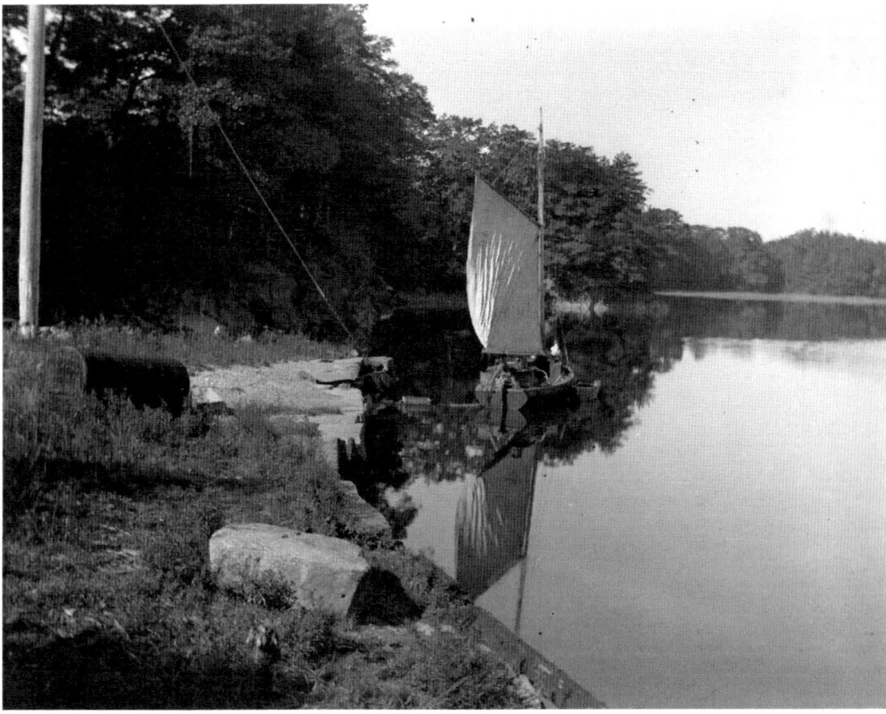

A sloop at a quarry dock on the Saco River, date unknown. *Robert H. Gay Photograph Collection, courtesy of McArthur Public Library.*

many men at various points in the process, employed the largest portion of Biddeford residents until the advent of textile mills in the area.[65] By the turn of the nineteenth century, the seventeen mills on the Saco River were cranking out fifty thousand feet of lumber per day.[66]

The majority of processed lumber was exported throughout the country and Europe, but Biddeford's shipbuilding industry kept local demand for lumber high. Near the falls and in the small village of Winter Harbor, various shipbuilding outfits utilized local lumber to craft a variety of vessels, including brigs, sloops, schooners and larger ships suitable for transatlantic travel and trade. Fishermen were the primary captains of these vessels, but they also served the trade industry along the waterways of the British colonies. What Vines identified as a safe harbor had quickly become a bustling seaport, and the area continues to serve as a home pier for many fishermen today.

In the days of developing commerce, Biddeford's residents fell into an economic hierarchy similar to that of the English villages from whence they came. Sailors who fished the local waterways and laborers who staffed

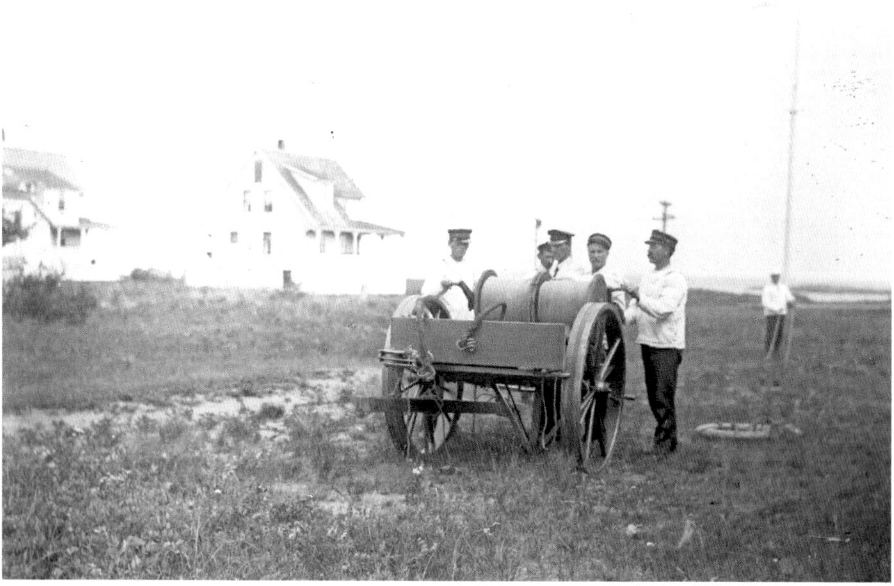

Coast Guard lifesavers with reel in Biddeford Pool, circa 1911. *Robert H. Gay Photograph Collection, courtesy of McArthur Public Library.*

the sawmills were among the lowest class. Small merchants, shopkeepers, artisans and farmers who populated areas closer to the falls and lived in decent dwellings were among members of the middle class. The greatest wealth of the community was among merchants, such as Pepperell and Cutts, who were joined by skilled professionals including lawyers, doctors, clergy and political figures, along with the few local aristocratic elite.[67] This social system was familiar to the early settlers and their subsequent generations of residents, which perpetuated this typical economic demographic structure as Biddeford continued to boom.

6
The River Defines

The population of Biddeford surpassed one thousand residents by the mid-eighteenth century. While a cluster of residents made their homes near the Saco River falls, many spread out on the acres to the east and west of the river, as well as downstream and at the mouth of the river in Winter Harbor. Despite the vast area in which residents lived, there remained but one meetinghouse for town gatherings and worship, situated to the west of the river halfway between the falls and Winter Harbor. Though ferry service made trips from the eastern riverbank to the western riverbank a bit easier, it was still treacherous to travel the distance for Sunday service, especially during inclement weather. With attendance required, some residents spent their entire Sunday traveling to and from and attending services, on what was surely their only day off after long, arduous hours of work.[68]

The residents to the eastern side of the river soon began a campaign for a second place of worship. Their pleas were heard, and permission was granted in 1752 to build a second meetinghouse. Pepperell donated the land for the structure, and construction began. It would take five years for the town to complete the meetinghouse, and then the struggle of obtaining a part-time minister began.[69]

Little did the residents realize at this point in time that "the division of the Biddeford parish was the first step toward a separate incorporation of the eastern half of the town."[70] Ten years after their petition for a second meetinghouse, "prominent citizens petitioned the General Court, showing 'that by reason of there being difficulties naturally attending the

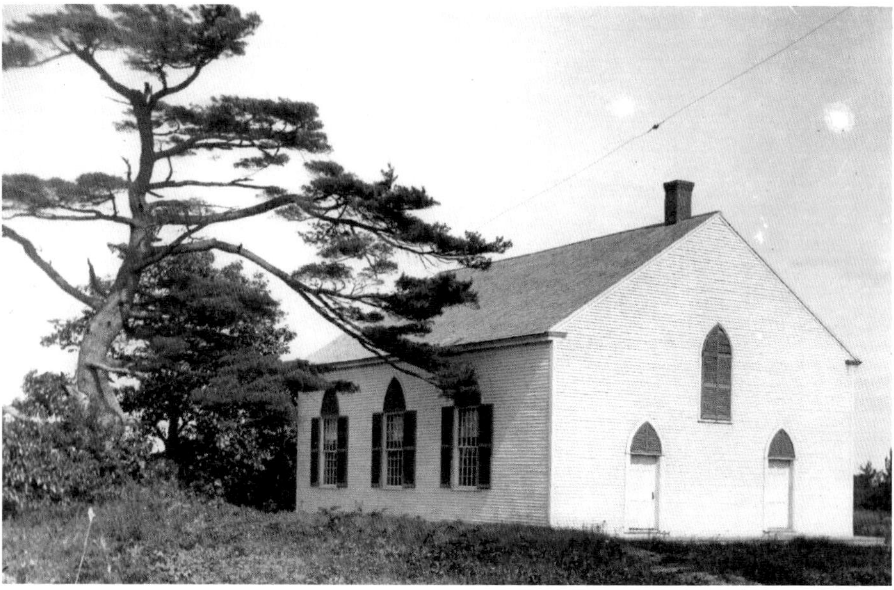

Still standing on the corner of Meeting House and Pool Roads, the First Parish Meetinghouse was the original meetinghouse for all of Biddeford and Saco prior to the settlement's division into two towns. It is pictured here circa 1910. *McArthur Public Library Archive.*

crossing said River…to attend to the necessary duty of public worship of God…that we should be separate'."[71] With that second plea, the residents were granted their petition to divide Biddeford where the river fell. The village on the eastern bank of the Saco River, with 540 residents, became Pepperellborough, named in honor of Sir William Pepperell. It would maintain this designation until 1805, when the town took the designation Saco through a reincorporation process. The area to the west of the river, with 629 residents, would forever retain the designation Biddeford.[72]

This division forced the remnants of Biddeford and the newly formed Pepperellborough to form local governing bodies of their own. However, the development of commerce blended throughout the subsequent decades. Equally talented craftsmen opened shops in the developing downtowns on either side of the river. Both towns attracted doctors, lawyers and merchants who established businesses downtown. The influx of upper-class citizens did not give pause to the laborers, and the lumber, shipbuilding and fishing industries continued to thrive. The Revolutionary War only briefly paused the progress of Biddeford's development. Historically in opposition to the British Parliament, Biddeford residents quickly joined in the throes of war seeking independence from England. Local representatives were sent

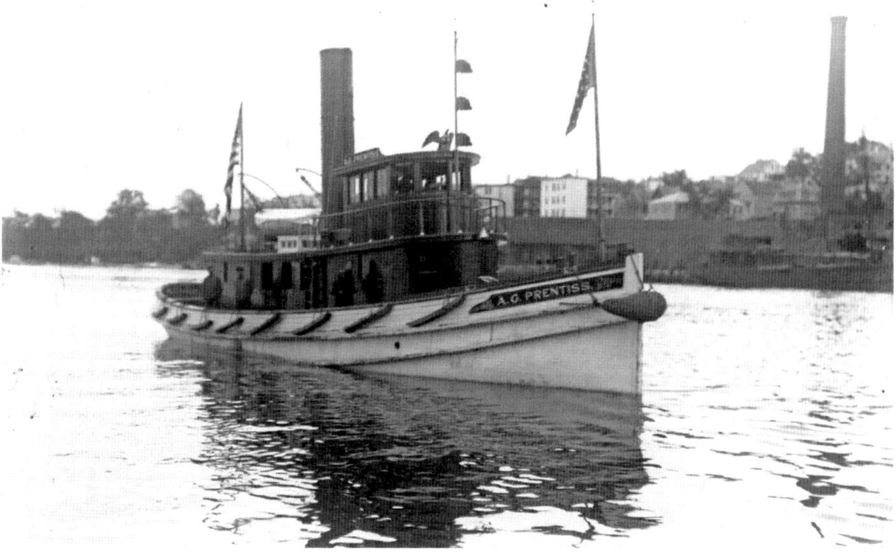

The tugboat *A.G. Prentiss* steams along the Saco River with the mill smokestack and residential tenements in the background, circa 1912. *McArthur Public Library Archive.*

to the Provincial Congress, and able-bodied men left Biddeford to join in combat. With the area's exposed waterways, local residents also took it upon themselves to remain alert to possible attacks. Such was the case with Captain Benjamin Hooper, a local seaman, who formed a patrol company to keep watch from Kennebunkport north to Saco.[73]

When the Declaration of Independence was signed on July 4, 1776, Biddeford residents celebrated with others in the newly free, and newly formed, United States of America. After this secession from England, more growth could be marked in Biddeford. It was evident that a center of commerce was developing near the river's rapid falls, creating a hub of activity in what would later become Biddeford's downtown district. Meanwhile, the area drew many a visitor who saw great potential in the area, including the believed-to-be first American female journalist, Anne Royall. She toured the area shortly after Maine's declaration as a state in 1820 and predicted it would become "one of the most flourishing towns in the state."[74] Her reports of the area were complimentary:

> *The bustle of the workmen, the noise of the numerous mills, etc., the view and roaring of the falls, render Saco a lively, delightful, and picturesque*

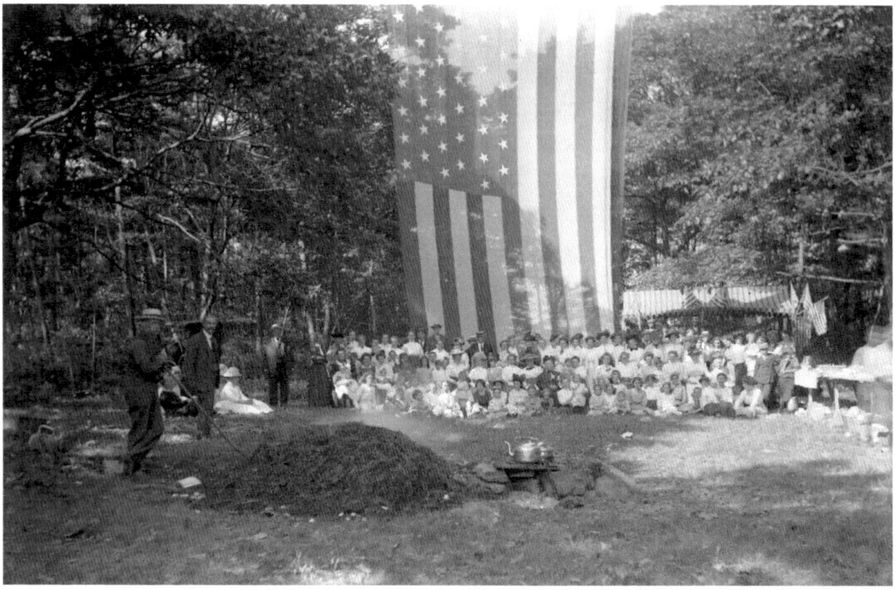

An annual reunion of "ancient and honorable of lower Biddeford" is celebrated with a clambake at Barley Field, circa 1912. *Robert H. Gay Photograph Collection, courtesy of McArthur Public Library.*

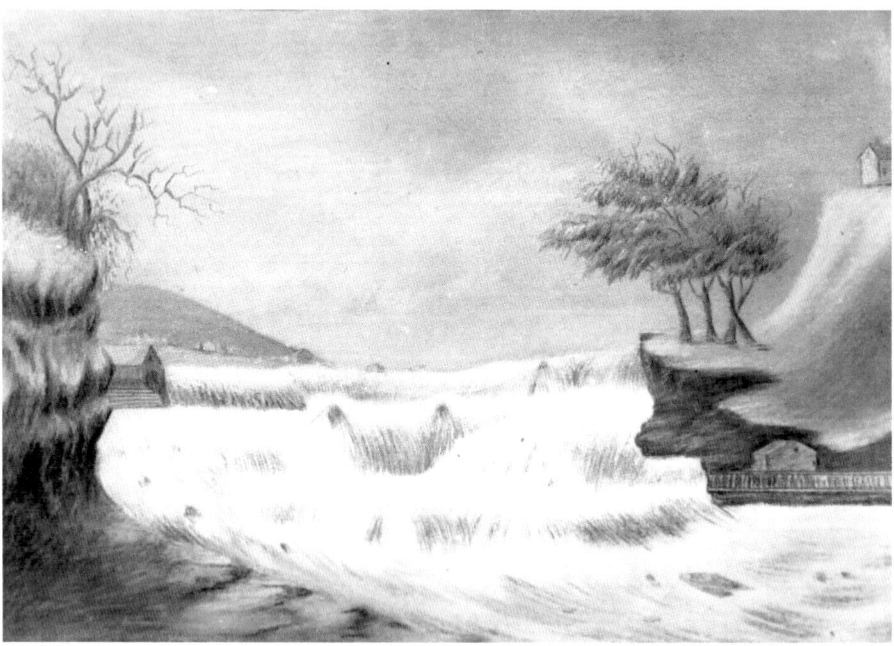

A painting of the Saco River falls prior to the introduction of textile mills along the river, circa 1829. *McArthur Public Library Archive.*

> *town. The scenery is by far the most handsome and variegated of any town in Maine. The land* [of Biddeford] *on the opposite shore being hilly and wooded—the falls in the center of town. It has a most wild and fanciful appearance. There are bridges over the Saco River at this place, connecting Biddeford and the shipping in the harbor, all adds to its beauty.*[75]

Among the mills Royall saw was an ironworks factory on Colonel Cutts's island. Built in 1811, the factory produced nearly 3,500 pounds of nails a day.[76] It was among one of the busiest mills in the area when Colonel Cutts died in 1821, leaving an estate valued at approximately $100,000 to his son Dominicus Cutts. Without much hesitation, Cutts's son posted his inheritance for sale. This sale would shift the course of Biddeford's industry in a new direction.

Part II

Industrializing the Falls

7
A New Kind of Mill

Although their loyalty to the United States was unquestionable, the citizens [of Maine] became restless under Massachusetts rule," and they pushed for independent statehood, which was achieved in 1820.[77] Concurrently, residents of Biddeford had recognized "the lumbering, shipbuilding, and brick making industries were not enough to support the [constantly growing] population."[78]

As if hearing the desperate call of Biddeford residents, an engineer and textile pioneer arrived. Samuel Batchelder first saw Saco River's powerful falls in 1831, shortly after Saco's first textile mill failed due to a fire that destroyed the business.[79] At the time, Batchelder was forty-seven, and his journey from Boston took two days by stagecoach. "Standing on the Biddeford bluffs where the ruins of the old stone fort were still visible, Batchelder was deeply impressed by the magnificent power of the hurling water."[80]

Batchelder was an innovator with experience in the textile mills of Lowell, Massachusetts. While more than two centuries of men had noticed the great value of the Saco River and the strategic positioning of both Biddeford and Saco as hubs for commerce, none had seen such great potential as did Batchelder. While sawmills dotted the river, the land immediately surrounding the falls had been preserved as pastures for local cattle—an underutilized resource, to Batchelder's innovative eye. Within a year's time of first laying eyes on those Biddeford bluffs, Batchelder had invested in land and erected the first textile mill on Saco Island.[81]

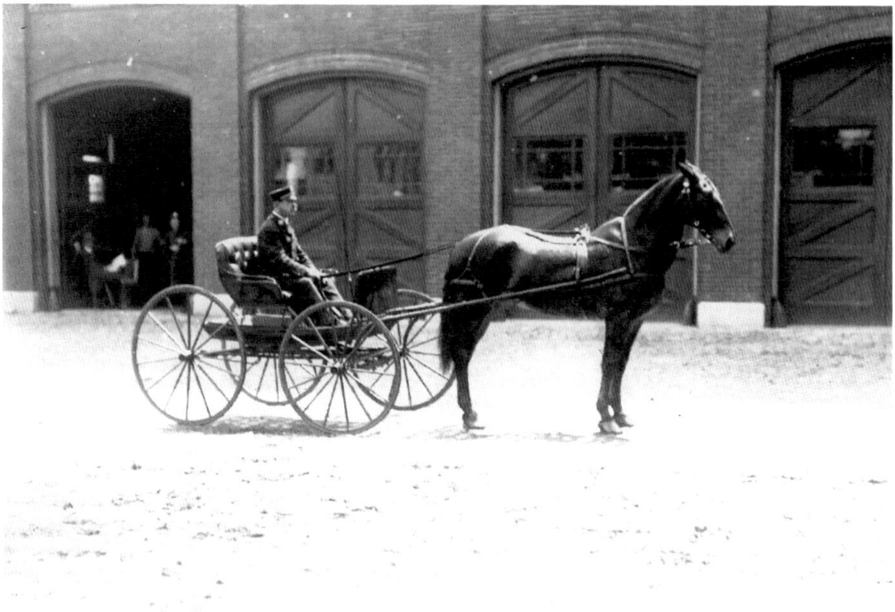

Biddeford Fire Department chief Charles H. Bonser in front of the fire station with the department's horse and buggy, circa 1913. *McArthur Public Library Archive.*

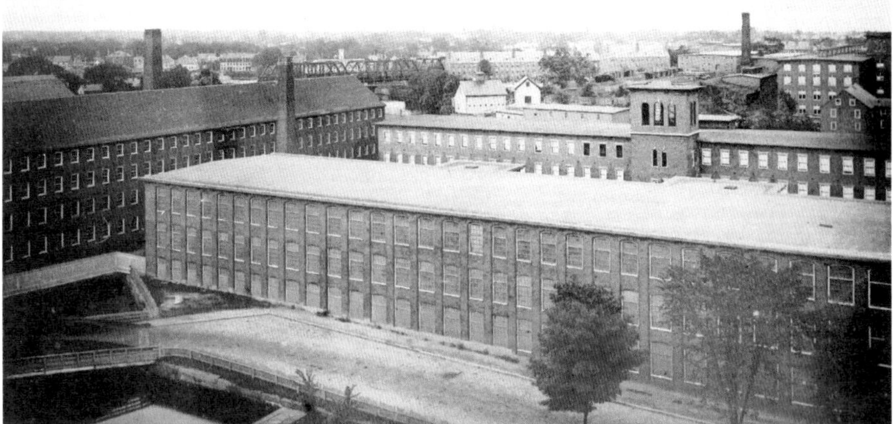

An eastward view of the Pepperell Manufacturing Company's buildings, circa 1894. *McArthur Public Library Archive.*

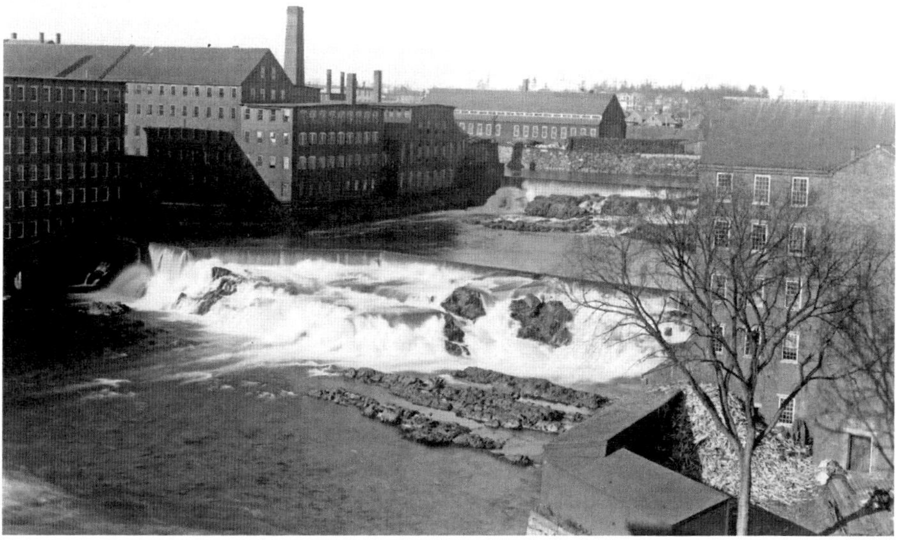

Above: The Saco Water Power Company along the Saco River falls, circa 1890, powered the mills along the river. *McArthur Public Library Archive*.

At this time in America's history, many necessary textiles were made at home. Early settlers brought with them their knowledge and skill of spinning fibers and weaving thread to produce cloth needed for linens and clothing. The separation from England had forced Americans to be more self-sufficient in many ways, prompting a need for more efficient production of cloth than the long, often tedious process of harvesting cotton or animal fibers (such as wool), cleaning, carding, spinning and weaving or knitting to produce garments needed in daily life. This concept of a textile mill in such a small village was foreign to Biddeford residents, who were still raising livestock, harvesting fields and continuing the productive lifestyle of their ancestors.[82]

However hesitant residents were to embrace Batchelder's vision, his entrepreneurial spirit and keen business drive would change the landscape and life in Biddeford over the course of the next century. The first textile mill on Saco Island took three years to prove successful, but once it did, the possibilities seemed limitless. By 1837, Batchelder chartered the Saco Water Power Company in order to harness the energy capacity that the rapid falls produced. In 1840, he obtained the title to land in Biddeford along the falls, and three years later, he broke ground on the first textile mill on the western riverbank.[83] Inspired by the previous landowner, Batchelder incorporated this upper mill division as Pepperell Manufacturing Company.[84]

When Batchelder first arrived, "Biddeford was then only a small village, almost wholly rural, and not even important enough to have its own post office."[85] Batchelder envisioned the newly incorporated Pepperell Manufacturing Company becoming the epicenter of commerce along the Saco River's falls, spurring growth in population and the economy. Without this confident vision, Biddeford could have easily remained a rural community:

> *When Samuel Batchelder began the mills at Biddeford, he changed the skyline, he increased the economic resources, he swelled the population. These changes bred other changes, equally marked. A broadening of mental and social horizons, an increase in living comforts, in actual joy of living, a swelling of interest and opportunities that affected an entire countryside.*[86]

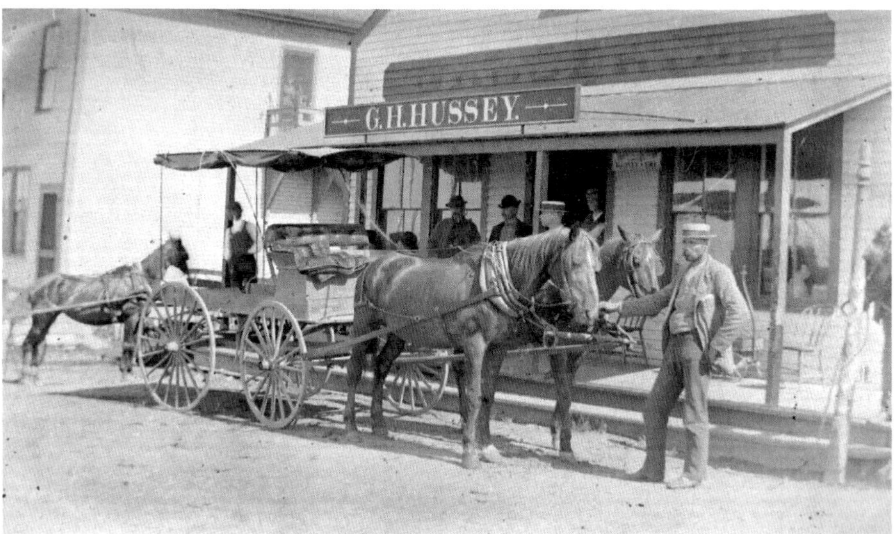

Mailman Oren Edwards pictured with his carriage in front of George H. Hussey's store and post office in Biddeford Pool, circa 1896. *McArthur Public Library Archive.*

8

The Girls Get to Work

Compared to modern-day standards, the development of Pepperell Manufacturing Company seems painfully slow. However, the business grew steadily, turned an increased profit annually and boosted the local economy immensely. The construction of new buildings necessitated mass quantities of lumber, brick and granite. As the first mill was built, "brickmaking, a long and profitable occupation in a clay-abundant terrain, underwent a revolution" to meet the demand.[87] Horse-powered machinery was introduced, helping local brickyards produce 10 million to 12 million bricks annually during the years mill buildings were erected.[88] The lumber industry also profited from these new buildings, as large beams were needed for framework and planks for flooring, features of which can be seen today in renovated mill buildings. Additionally, local quarries hauled granite from the woods to the developing downtown to be used for foundations.[89]

As mill buildings were slowly constructed and machinery manufactured at local machine shops was brought in, staffing was needed in mass quantity to spin fibers and weave cloth. In 1845, Batchelder ran a job advertisement seeking hardworking employees. The ad copy promised a weekly salary of $1.50 to $3.00 a week plus room and board for women in clean, spacious company boardinghouses.[90] At the time, women working in New York City earning top dollar made $4.00 a week, making Batchelder's offer quite generous.[91] The prospect of steady work for steady wages appealed to women living in the rural reaches of Maine. Young, unmarried ladies "braved the dangers of rickety stages, deep mud, and high waters to venture down the

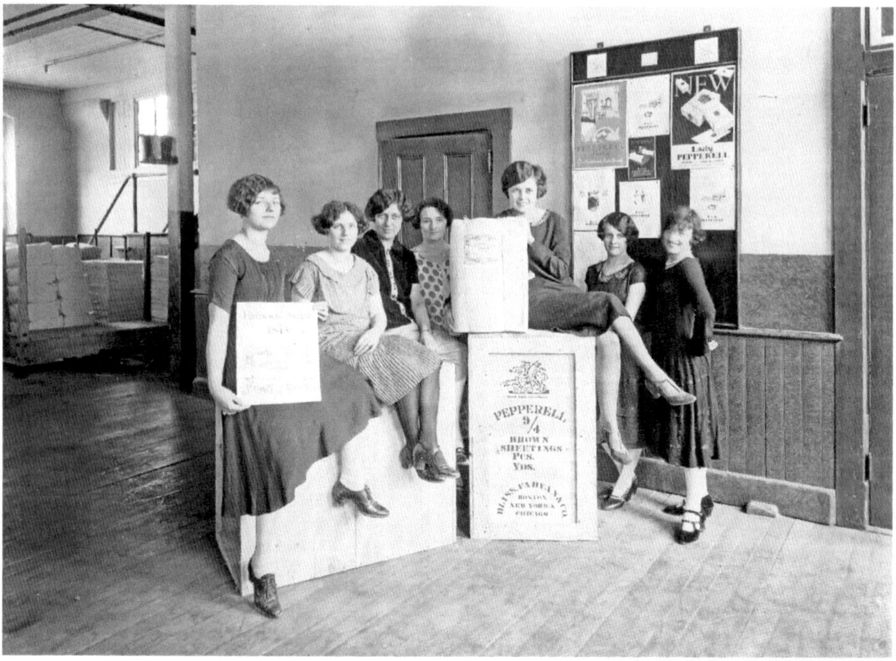

A group of packaging room employees poses with bales and cases prior to products being shipped. The Pepperell Manufacturing Company's famous dragon insignia can be seen branded on the side of the crate. *McArthur Public Library Archive.*

Saco Valley to tend the spindles and looms," arriving in droves over the next few decades.[92]

In addition to new mills, the company built boardinghouses on its twelve acres of property. These tenements were within walking distance to the mills, ensuring girls could easily make it to work on time and return home safely. The girls worked ten- to twelve-hour days and early on were required to abide by a 10:00 p.m. curfew. The girls were under supervision twenty-four hours a day; mill agents kept close watch on everyone at work, and housemothers kept an eye on their well-being at the boardinghouses.[93] Free housing coupled with their weekly salary "often enabled a girl to help pay off her father's mortgage, assist a relative, or build a secure basis for her own marriage."[94]

These young ladies, who previously worked the fields of their family's farms, helped their mothers maintain a household and had experience with weaving garments from sheep's wool, learned their job roles quickly. Openers and pickers opened the cotton and cleaned the fibers of seeds, stems and leaves. Carders continued the cleaning process while beginning to straighten the fibers. Lap winders created batting from the cotton before railway heads formed the fleece into soft rolls. Drawing frames, speeders, and extensors combined, straightened, drew out and started to twist the fibers. Warp frames continued the stretching and spinning process before the thread was wound onto bobbins. The thread on bobbins was transferred to the weaving room, where it was finally transformed into fabric. The whole manufacturing cycle "seems [like] simple processes, but there was great difficulty in keeping the machines running without interruption so the cotton cloth could be produced cheaply."[95] Of course, it was the mill girls' goal to ensure production did not stop, because the faster cloth was produced, the faster Pepperell Manufacturing Company would grow to become an international textile powerhouse.

9
Business Grows

The arrival of girls who worked in the mills boosted Biddeford's population in 1848 to five thousand. Of the town's residents, two thousand were employees of Pepperell Manufacturing Company. This was the largest population boom in the town's history to date, and the numbers continued to grow steadily, as would the textile company.

With staff in place working long hours six days a week, Pepperell Manufacturing Company quickly turned a profit and would continue to do so throughout the remainder of the century. With the success of his business and his advancing age, Batchelder saw the need to create a board of directors to manage the company. Pepperell Manufacturing Company's incorporating executives included head of finance William Dwight, registered agent William P. Haines and merchandiser Francis Skinner. Dwight's first task was to raise $1 million by selling 2,000 shares to support the continued growth of the company. With the advent of the gold rush and many businessmen pursuing financial opportunities on the frontier, Dwight struggled to sell shares. Frustrated with the work it took to obtain ninety-nine investors, he named himself the one-hundredth, claiming 664 shares valued at $382,000.[96]

With financial backing, it then was Skinner's job, as proprietor of the merchandising firm Francis Skinner and Company of Boston, which was appointed to handle the textile company's sales, to market Pepperell Manufacturing Company products. Considered "a man ahead of his times in business ideals," Skinner insisted that "products be sold 'purely on quality'" and not just for the best price.[97] He made it his primary goal to please even the pickiest of American women and to persuade them to choose Pepperell Manufacturing Company products over other cloth because of the value in its quality. He insisted on personally inspecting each sample before approving its mass production:

> *Even today,* [the managers of Pepperell Manufacturing Company] *form an intensely interesting case history of a mill whose product was planned, brought into being and its quality set by a superbly market-wise mind thinking only in terms of quality merchandising—and before ever a yard of cloth appeared in a difficult market.*[98]

In Lowell, Massachusetts, Batchelder began his textile career with the invention of drill, a durable cotton fabric with a strong bias in the weave. He made drill Pepperell Manufacturing's first product, but Skinner perfected it

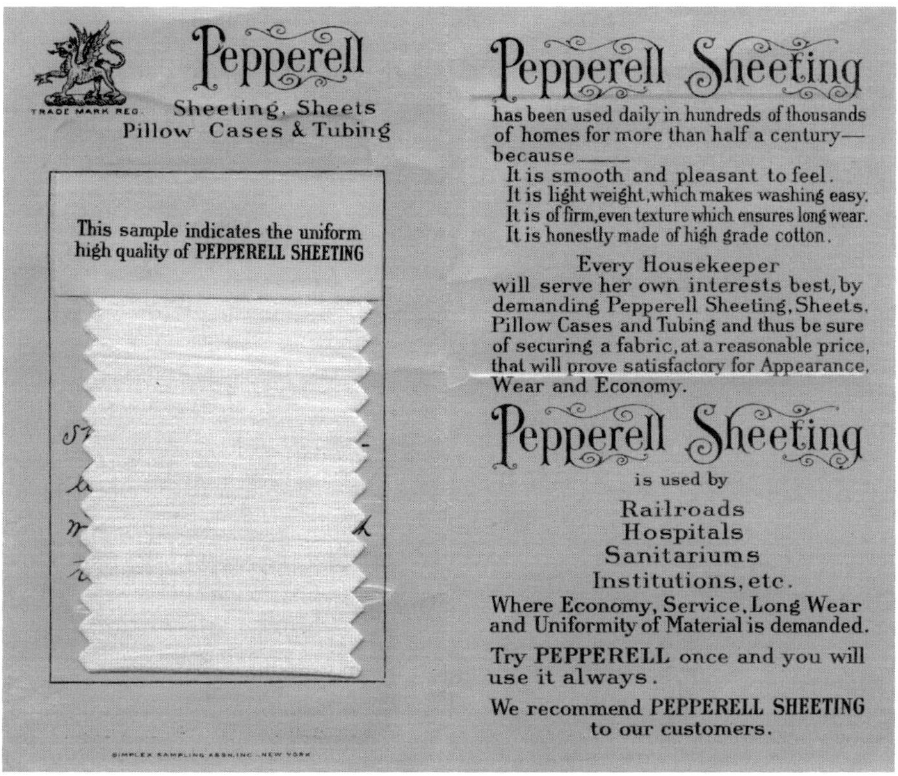

A 1910 sales brochure from Farley, Harvey and Company featuring two Pepperell Manufacturing Company fabric samples. *Richard N. Carr Collection, courtesy of McArthur Public Library.*

to meet his scrupulous standards. After testing a litany of samples, Skinner approved the refined quality and cleared it for production. Pepperell Manufacturing Company finally released its first product in 1851, selling the cloth for six to nine cents a yard depending on the width of the bolt. Within a year, Skinner obtained an order from Boston export firm Dane, Dana and Company for 1,100 bales (more than 650,000 yards)—enough to cover approximately 125 miles. The export firm reordered the same amount before the year's end.[99]

With the company's core product a success, Skinner turned his attention to branding. He hired a Boston artist to assist with the creation of a logo that would represent Pepperell Manufacturing Company as an international brand. The logo needed to be culturally acceptable for customers as far east as China, recognizable and regal. Skinner used the images of Chinese dragons and those found on the crest of English Tudors as inspiration for the Pepperell dragon. For customers who could not read the English printed on the packaging, the logo "was accepted by the teeming millions of China and the far East…no imitation ever long deceived [their] keen and sharp memories."[100] The artist who created the Pepperell dragon is unknown, but the company's ledger noted a fourteen-dollar expense for the drawing, an expense that proved to be well worth the investment for decades to come.[101] The dragon became synonymous with the company's products, which were recognized internationally for their unmatched quality. By 1856, the company's sales surpassed $1 million.[102]

10

Shevenell's Journey

The unprecedented growth and success of Pepperell Manufacturing Company created a seemingly endless source of work in Biddeford through the twentieth century. That promise of plentiful work enticed many to Biddeford over the course of fifty years, especially the French Canadians. According to his descendants, Israel Shevenell was the first French Canadian to arrive in Biddeford and find work. In the spring of 1845, at just nineteen years old, Shevenell walked two hundred miles from his hometown of Compton, Quebec. According to his great-great-great-granddaughter Tonya Shevenell, his likely route took him through the White Mountains and along the Saco River. He quickly found work at one of the brickyards, rapidly turning out bricks for the textile mills under construction along the river. He earned three dollars a week through the summer and into the fall before returning to Quebec. Shevenell returned the following summer to find more work available. The following year, he convinced his family to immigrate to Biddeford with him to make it their permanent residence.[103]

The story of Israel Shevenell's first encounter and eventual relocation to Biddeford is not an anomaly. The immigration of French Canadians started as a trickle; lone men traveled south for seasonal work to supplement their families' income. This soon fostered a desire to relocate the entire family for year-round employment. This trend marked a new kind of immigration not before seen in colonial settlements. Previously, European men traveled across the Atlantic alone, seeking adventure and often traveling beyond the colonial settlements westward to explore the new frontier. Since the early colonial

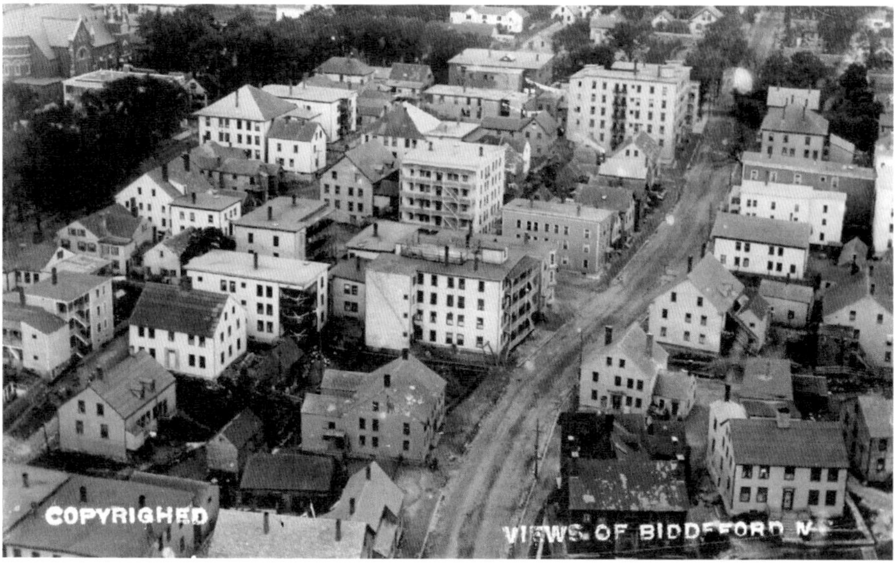

An aerial view of lower Hill Street with St. Andre's Church in the upper left corner. *Richard N. Carr Collection, courtesy of McArthur Public Library.*

days, it was rare for whole families to arrive and settle in a community to start anew. However, this would become the history of the French Canadians as they moved en masse to find work while maintaining a closeness of the secular family cherished by their culture.[104]

The arrival of French Canadians came during an interesting period of American history. The North and the South had begun the Civil War. A story in the local newspaper entitled "Home Pictures of the Times," though fictional, describes a common scene as a boy named Walter tells his sister Lottie, "I'm young and brave and strong, but my country needs me now, and I should be ashamed not to be ready in the hour of her need and peril."[105] That fictional boy was like many real teenagers, young adults and older men answering the call to serve the Yankee cause. This created a strain on the mill workforce, which was quickly defrayed by French Canadians arriving ready to work. Pepperell Manufacturing Company quickly welcomed immigrants, who filled vacated positions and aided in the survival of Biddeford's textile industry.

It was not long before mill agents developed a fondness for the French Canadian work ethic. Most of these immigrants were accustomed to working on farms, which required twelve-hour days and extensive physical labor. Additionally, the whole family was willing to work:

> *Women worked the looms and carding and filling machines. They kept a close watch on moving threads, replaced bobbins and made quick ties when thread broke. This was physically taxing work, which required constant alertness. The men performed the heavier labor, including preparing the machines, pushing cotton filled carts from room to room, and general maintenance work....* [O]*ver seventy percent of the children between the ages of ten and fourteen were working in the mills.*[106]

This work ethic helped Pepperell Manufacturing Company continue to thrive during the Civil War while other mills folded. The *Bath Times* reported, "the Brunswick cotton mill is to stop operations, the stock of cotton on hand promising larger profits to the owners by selling it in the raw state."[107] Biddeford mills did face some struggle, as the supply of Southern cotton was tied up in the ongoing war between the North and South.

While Maine was not the primary battleground for the Civil War, it did contribute a lot of men to the armed forces. For that reason, local newspapers focused heavily on war coverage. Weekly editions of the *Union and Journal*

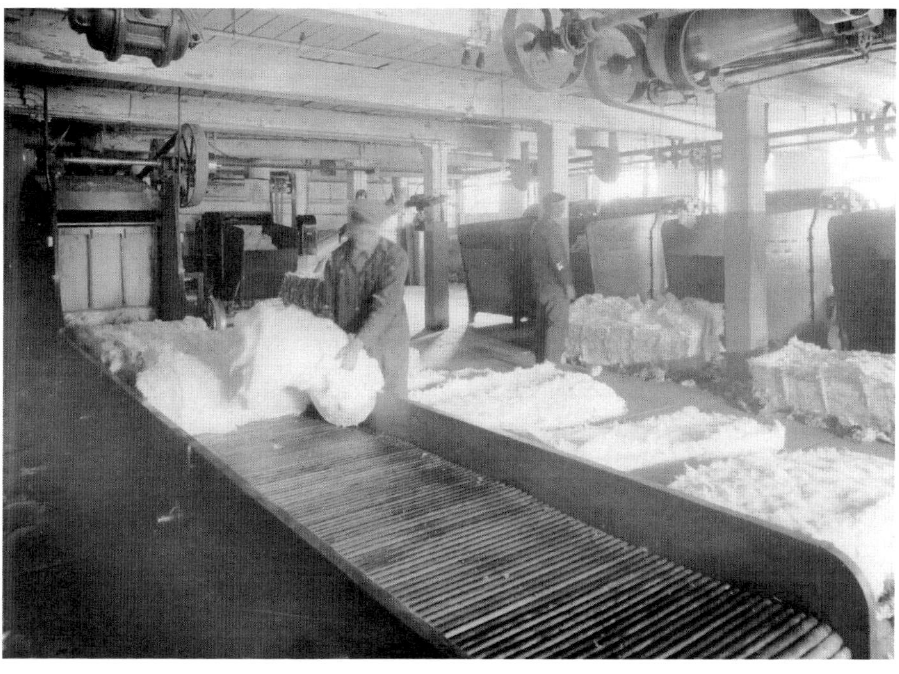

Pepperell Manufacturing Company employees breaking apart bales of cotton, circa 1925. This was the first step in processing cotton into thread and fabric. *McArthur Public Library Archive.*

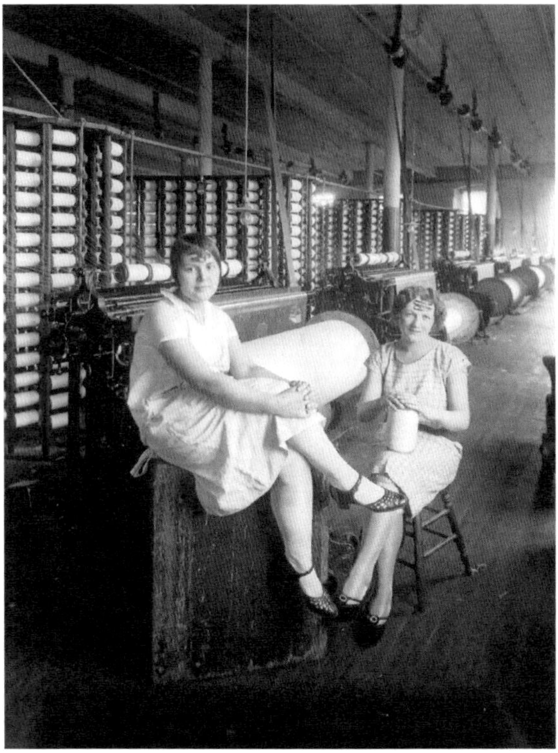

Left: Two warp room employees at the Pepperell Manufacturing Company pose in front of their machines, circa 1925. *McArthur Public Library Archive.*

Opposite, top: A group of spool room employees at the Pepperell Manufacturing Company pose for a photo, circa 1925. *McArthur Public Library Archive.*

Opposite, bottom: Prior to packaging for sale, the cloth produced by Pepperell Manufacturing Company was closely inspected by staff to ensure its quality. *McArthur Public Library Archive.*

Below: Two spinning room employees at the Pepperell Manufacturing Company pose in front of their machines, circa 1925. *McArthur Public Library Archive.*

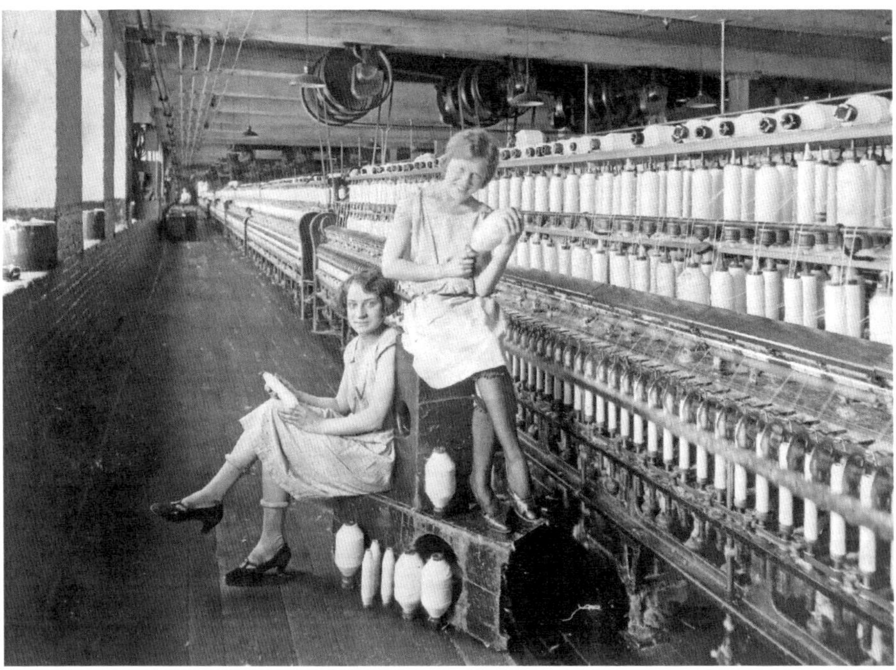

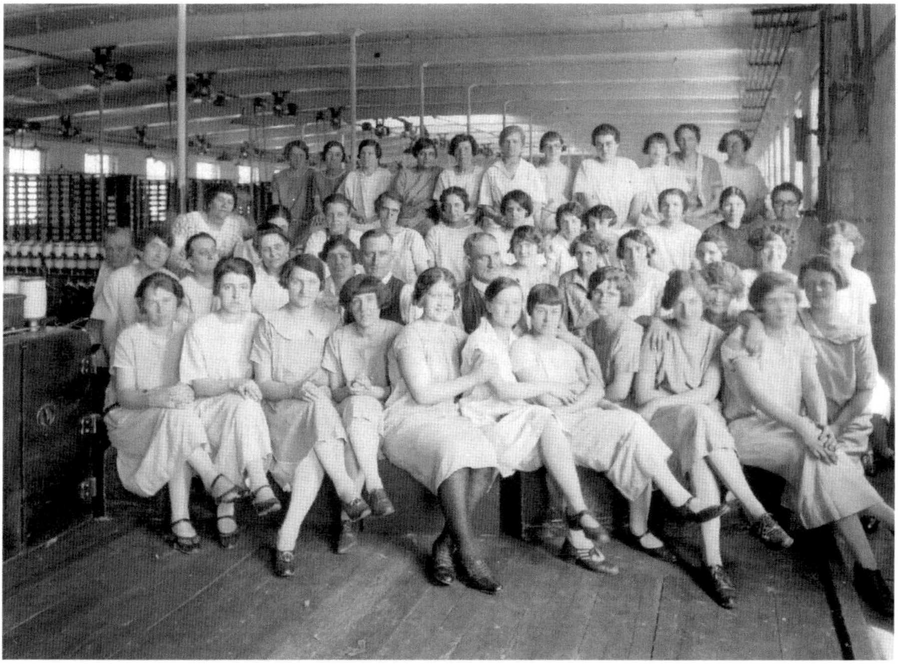

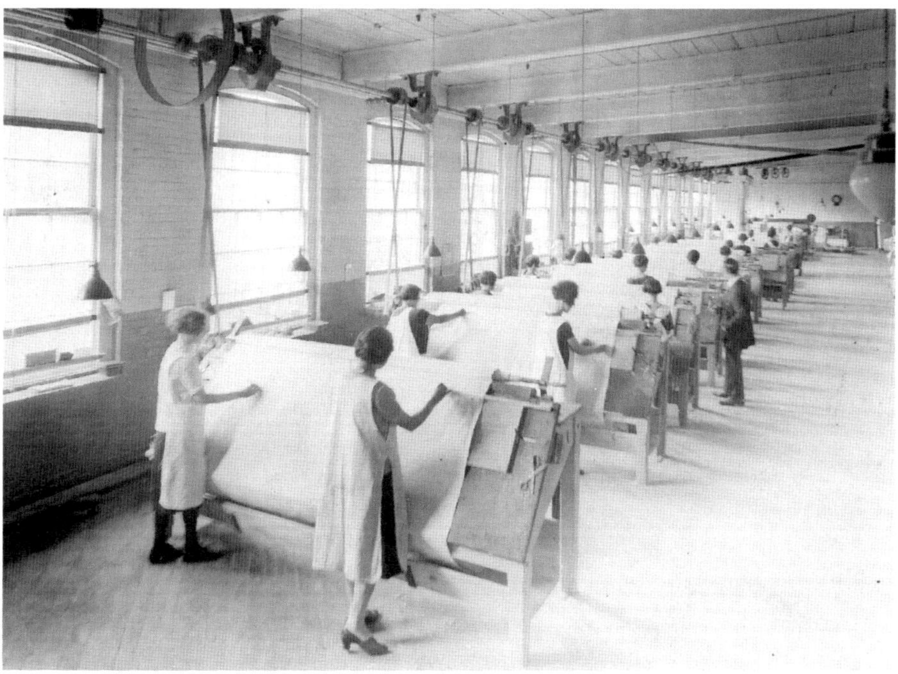

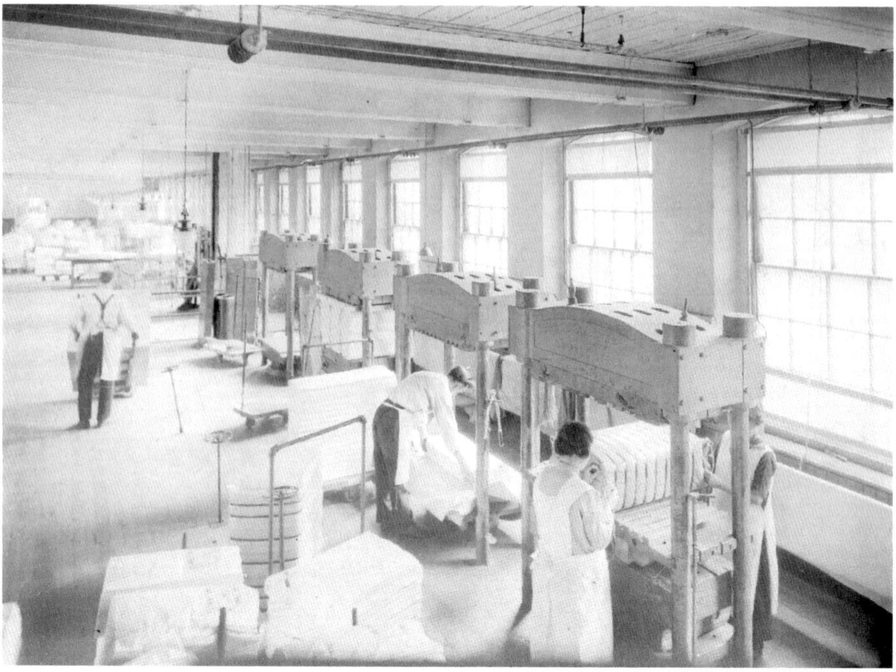

Cloth balers prepare the products of Pepperell Manufacturing Company for packaging. *McArthur Public Library Archive.*

published regular columns throughout the war reporting on politics and outcomes of various battles. Compared to the American Revolution and other European wars, this type of war coverage was unprecedented and garnered much interest from local readers.[108]

Many editions featured letters from soldiers received by local families. A Biddeford girl submitted one letter from her brother, identified only as George, dated May 5, 1862. In the letter, he wrote:

> *Here we were to disembark our troops and take the forts by storm, but the enemy perceiving our intention and knowing that the city was already in our hands...very wisely concluded to surrender before we landed one quarter of our forces.*[109]

Working men and women in Biddeford remained engaged in the ongoing war efforts. Millworkers were inherently involved through weaving cloth for soldiers' uniforms, and local events helped educate the public about the battles. For example, an artistically rendered panorama of a battle scene was brought to the city for all to view. The *Union and Journal* reported that a "large and attentive audience" turned out for the event. The article stated, "The [panorama's] views were remarkably life-like, and represented the different modes to which men resort for the purpose of annihilating each other. It is worthy the patronage of all, wherever exhibited."[110]

When General Lee surrendered on April 9, 1865, Northerners breathed a sigh of relief. Six days later, they were shocked to learn of President Abraham Lincoln's assassination. An article published three days later in the *Maine Democrat* stated, "Words utterly fail to give an idea of the chill of horror which fell on all our hearts."[111] The bells rang throughout the city for an hour at noon. American flags dropped to half-mast. Though citizens were deeply saddened by the death of the country's leader, the end of the Civil War marked a new era not only nationwide, but also for Biddeford.

11
French Canadian Invasion

Between the end of the Civil War and the turn of the twenty-first century, Biddeford's population ballooned. According to census data, when Shevenell first arrived, Biddeford's population was approximately 2,574. By 1900, the population had increased to 16,145. By this time, three out of five residents in Biddeford were French Canadian, and these immigrants were responsible for 80 percent of the city's new births.[112]

In the early days of French Canadian immigration, mill agents advertised available jobs in Canada. However, word of mouth quickly replaced the need for advertising. The driving factor behind the rapid immigration comes down to the fact that French Canadians were coming to Biddeford en masse with their siblings, parents, grandparents, aunts, uncles and cousins. Entire extended families moved based on the promise of abundant work opportunities.

Unlike the mill girls of the mid-nineteenth century who lived in mill housing, these immigrants moved into apartments and rented houses. Entire families filled whole tenements or lived within a block of each other. The sheer quantity of French Canadians within a very small area of Biddeford's downtown became a domineering presence. An area settled by Englishmen and populated by western Europeans was now suddenly turning into Little Canada. French became the area's predominant language; it was spoken in homes and at work and was taught to children in school. Whereas past immigrants assimilated to American culture rather quickly, the French Canadian population resisted the idea. They held on to their cultural values

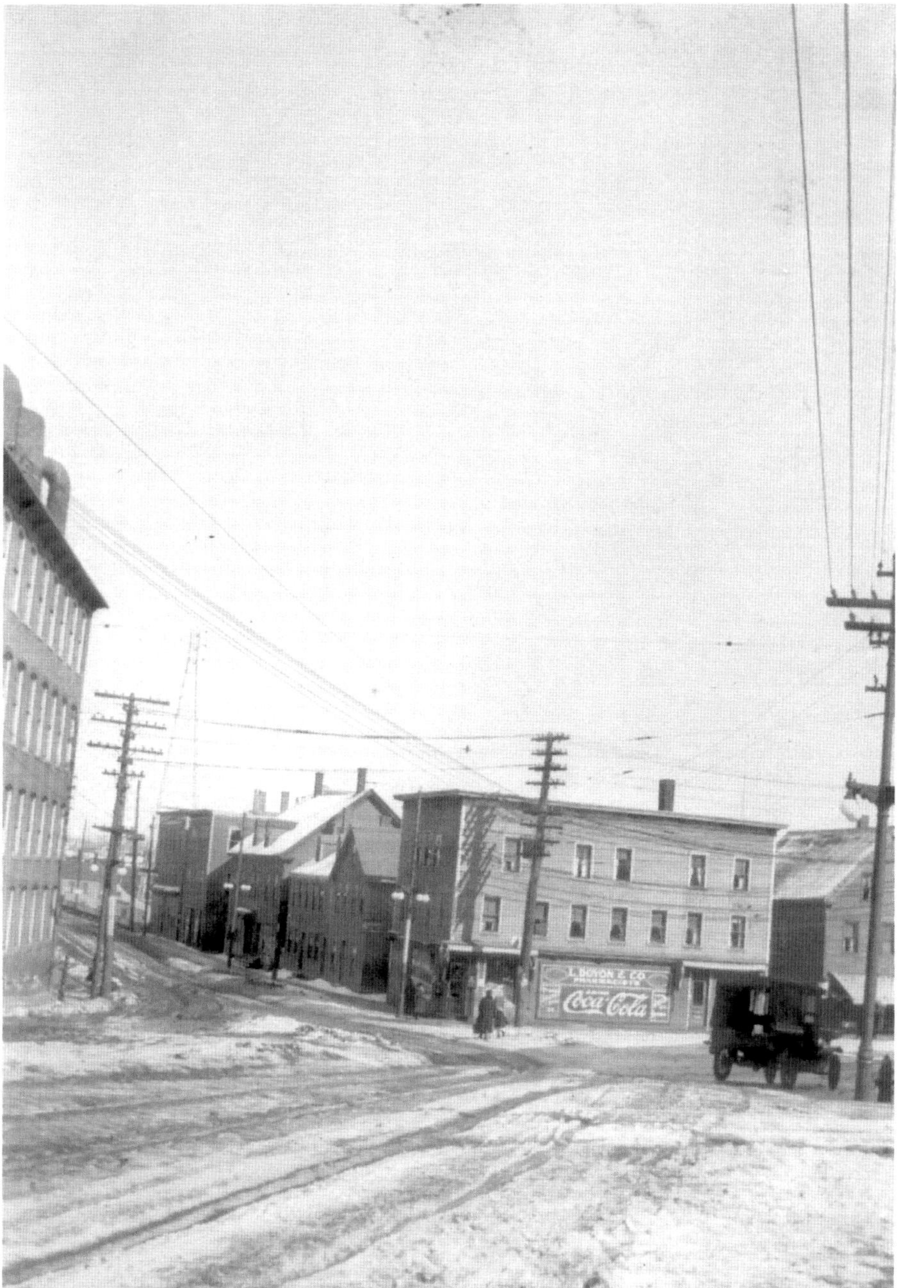

This view of Main Street features Doyon's Pharmacy, the intersection of Water Street and buildings on Factory Island, as well as the Pepperell Manufacturing Company mills to the left. *McArthur Public Library Archive.*

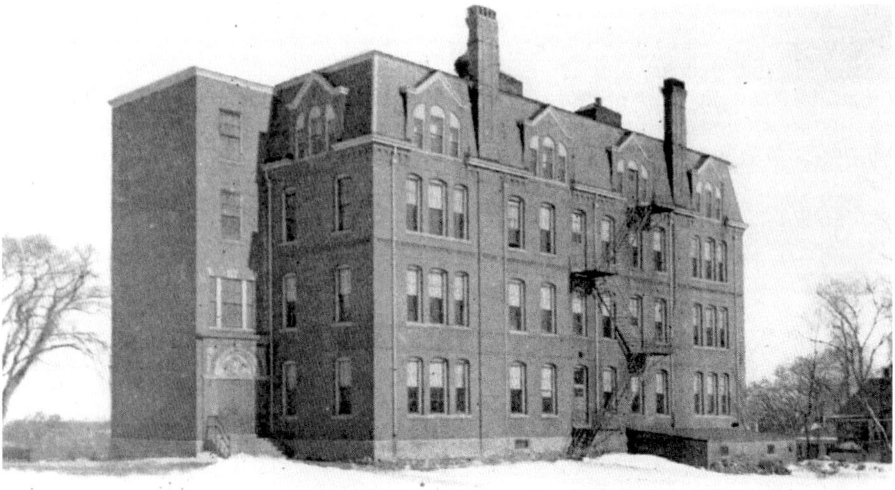

St. Joseph's School, a parochial school, pictured circa 1945, continues to educate youth in the same location today. The school, now St. James, continues to honor the Catholic faith. *McArthur Public Library Archive.*

easily because like-minded individuals surrounded them. Cultural social clubs were organized. The sudden demand for a Catholic parish prompted the founding and construction of St. Joseph Parish on Elm Street and the latter addition of St. Andre Church on Bacon Street. Many French Canadian traditions were upheld in both the home and the community.[113]

This resistance to assimilation was met with disapproval from families of European descent who were equally set in their ways. This caused tension within the city, despite affable interactions between the long-standing families of Biddeford and the newly arrived members of the community. When "one looks behind these formal proclamations of ethnic amity, however, one finds that Biddeford was also infected with the nativism that plagued other Maine cities."[114] Franco-Americans were "disparaged in private because of general dislike."[115] General dislikes morphed into blind hatred at times, often fueled by the looming fear of a work shortage in the mills.

The trend of French Canadian immigrants, dubbed Franco-Americans, filling vacated positions in the mill continued well past the end of the Civil War. When the Knights of Labor formed a chapter in Biddeford, the group organized a labor strike to protest low wages, long hours and dangerous work conditions. The Franco-Americans refused to join their counterparts in the strike and continued working while the picket line marched on. Rather than acknowledge the strike, mill agents hired more Franco-Americans to

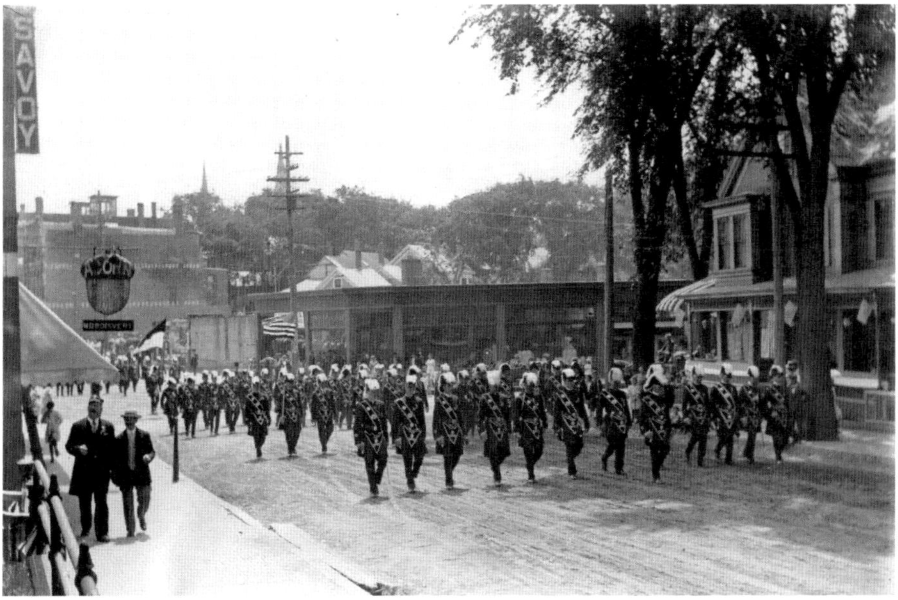

The Bradford Commandery of the Knights Templar, a Christian-oriented fraternal organization, participates in a parade on upper Main Street, circa 1915. *Robert H. Gay Photograph Collection, courtesy of McArthur Public Library.*

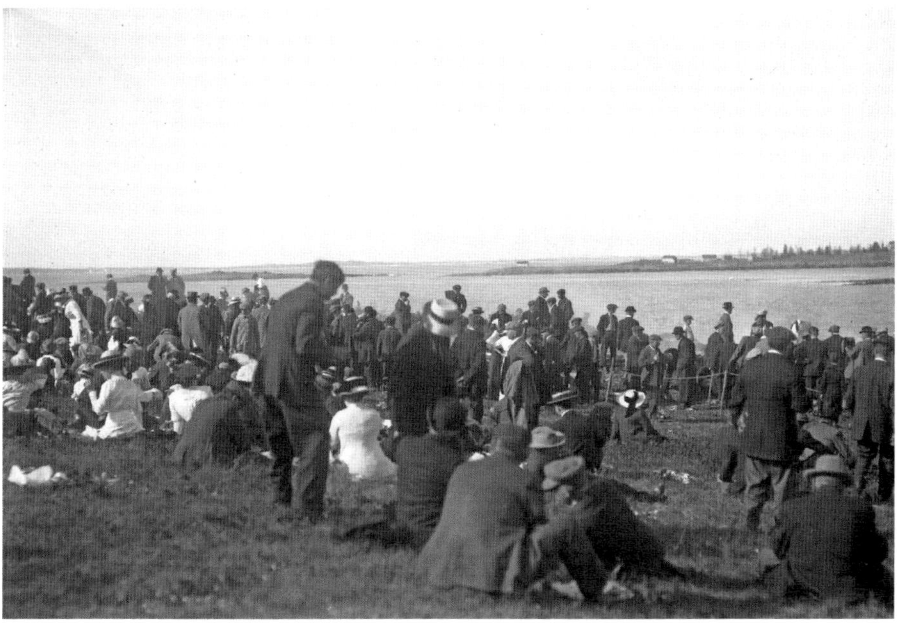

Members of the Knights Templar disembark from the *Pilgrim*, a steamer that traveled the Saco River, to enjoy Biddeford Pool on St. John's Day. *McArthur Public Library Archive.*

fill the empty positions left by the labor movement, further perpetuating animosity toward the immigrants.[116]

Concurrently, the Franco-Americans continued to dominate the community and continued to shirk assimilation. Many did not bother to learn English or encourage their children to learn English. Parishioners of St. Joseph Parish funded the founding of a parochial school, where French was taught and spoken. The relationship between immigrants and existing residents of Biddeford continued to be divisive. The introduction of more immigrants from Canada, England, Ireland, Greece and beyond created a diverse community divided by culture of origin. Decades passed before the tension between different cultural groups eased in Biddeford, but not before an encounter with the Ku Klux Klan in the 1920s.[117]

Opposite: Attendees wearing the height of fashion attend a lawn party at a residence in Biddeford Pool to raise funds in support of the war effort, circa 1917. *Robert H. Gay Photograph Collection, courtesy of McArthur Public Library.*

12

Growth and Caution

Rapid population growth naturally drove an increased demand for commerce in both Biddeford and Saco. Newspapers began featuring advertisements for various entrepreneurial ventures within the downtowns. As the years progressed, advertisements became more prevalent and more detailed.

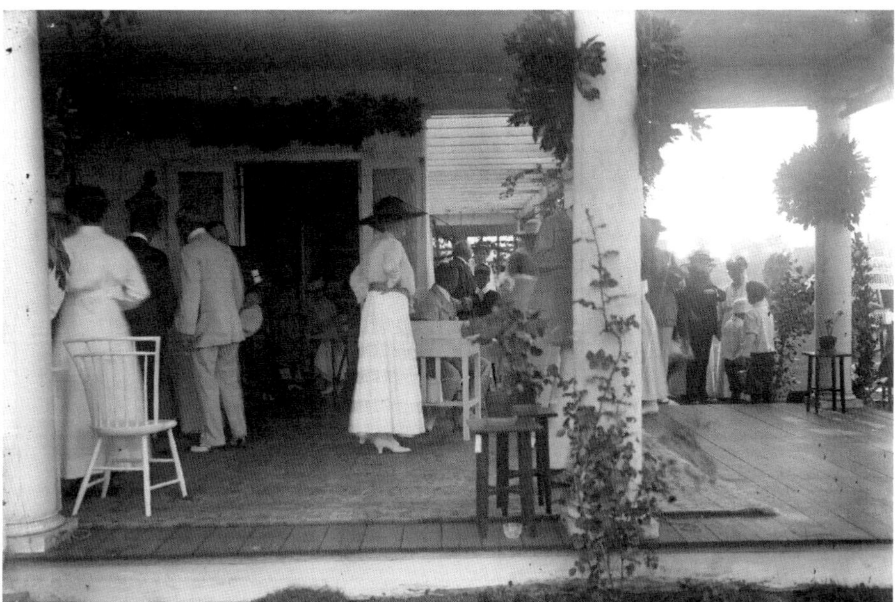

The *Maine Democrat*, a newspaper distributed in the area between 1828 and 1878, encouraged readers to visit shops and boutiques downtown, most boasting various frivolities. Shaw & Clark's newly opened store ran an advertisement on January 4, 1853, promising to "sell watches, clocks, jewelry, and fancy goods, at prices to suit customers or they will not be urged to purchase."[118] At Misses Bowdoin's shop one could find "New York styles" and rich millinery or lace goods. M&H Pierce offered "ornamental cakes" starting at 37.5 cents per pound, pleading, "Call in ladies at either of our offices in Saco or Biddeford, and let us show you the Cake, so that you may know where to buy when *your time* comes." Many of these advertisements appealed to readers with expendable funds. Many did not have the opportunity to shop regularly in the higher-end stores, but some saved up for special purchases.

The ad copy was dispersed among the pages of newsprint, and the type in between captured readers with interesting stories and practical advice. The paper ran columns to offer farmers tips based on the season. Women

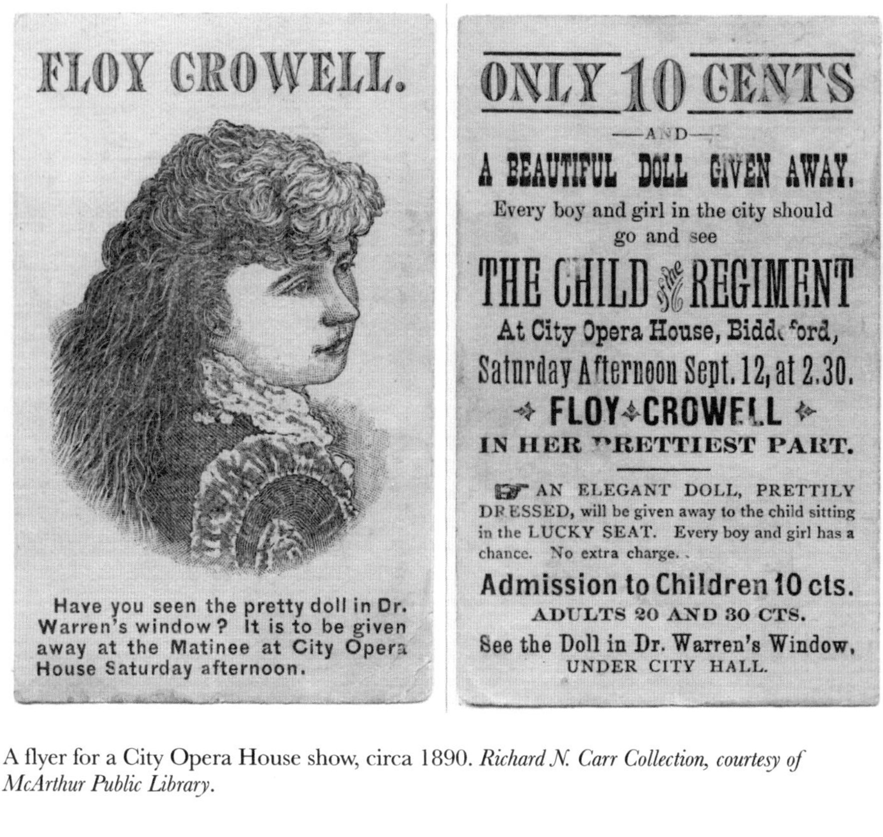

A flyer for a City Opera House show, circa 1890. *Richard N. Carr Collection, courtesy of McArthur Public Library.*

could read helpful instruction on maintaining a home or cooking. These columns often appeared without a byline and were based on little research. However, snippets capture the area's history, with birth, marriage and death briefs; police logs similar to what we see today; and accounts from the county commissioner.

Headlines were quick and catchy, and larger bold font was used to draw the reader to specific stories. "Fast Youth" was one headline on January 18, 1853, which prophesied "boys are nearly an extinct race. There is scarcely an intermediate stage between diapers and desperadoism."[119] The author continued to muse about children—both boys and girls—who seem to be growing up quickly compared to prior generations. Some of this speculation could be attributed to the fact that many children and teenagers entered the workforce at the textile mills alongside their parents, aunts and uncles.

The next week's newspaper pointed readers to a commissioner's report, which was heavily editorialized by the writer, who pointed first to the commissioner's "lengthy refutation" that "our course towards the Indians has been marked with injustice and inhumanity." The report notes how tribes were forced to the north and west after the French and Indian Wars, but the

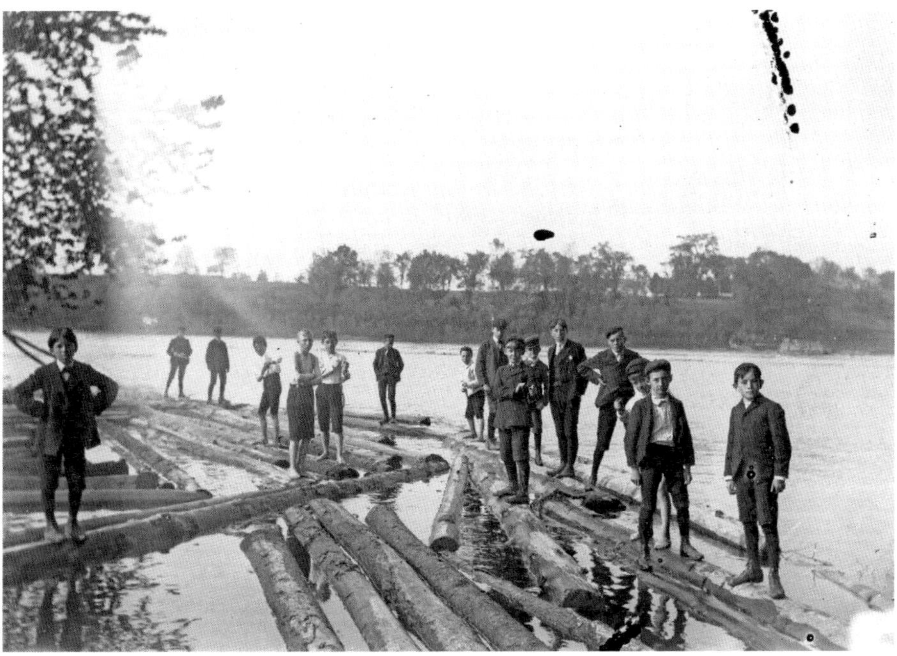

City boys on logs near outer South Street, circa 1911. *McArthur Public Library Archive.*

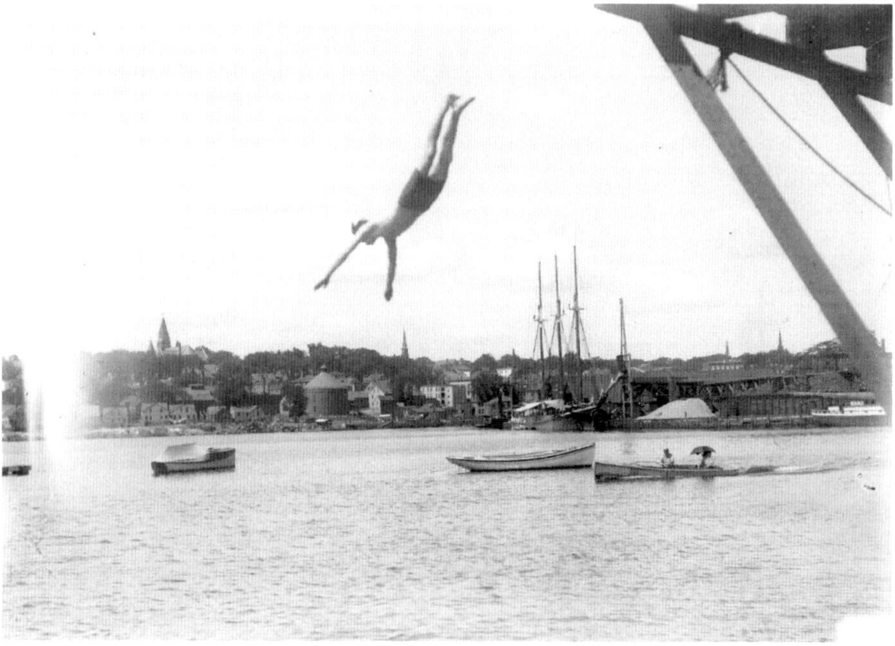

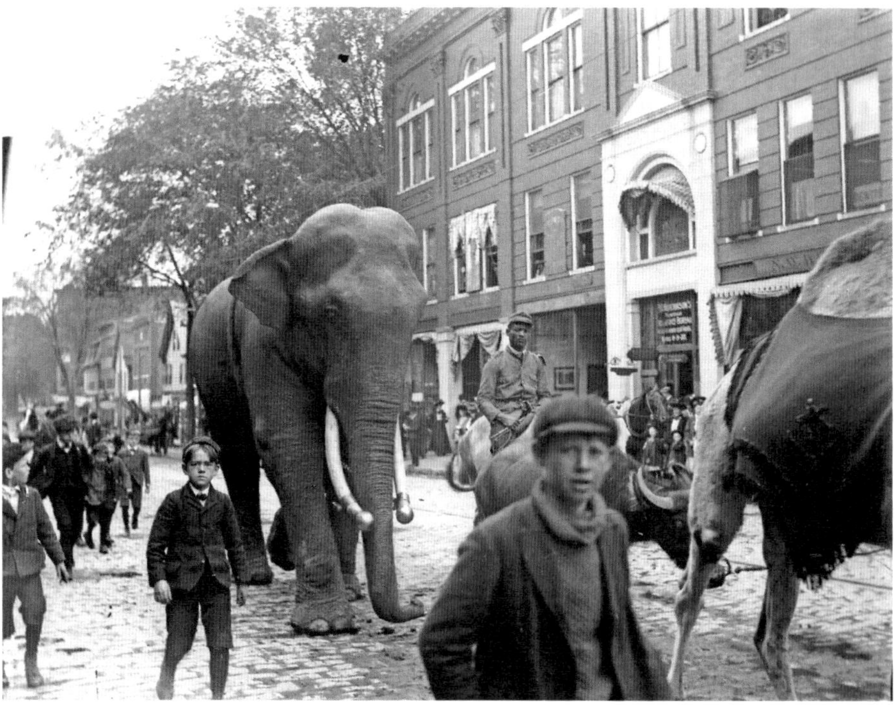

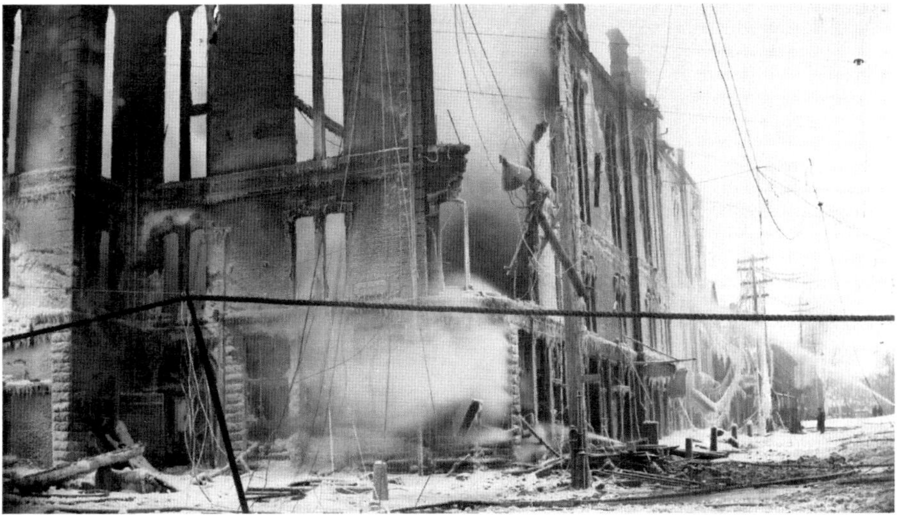

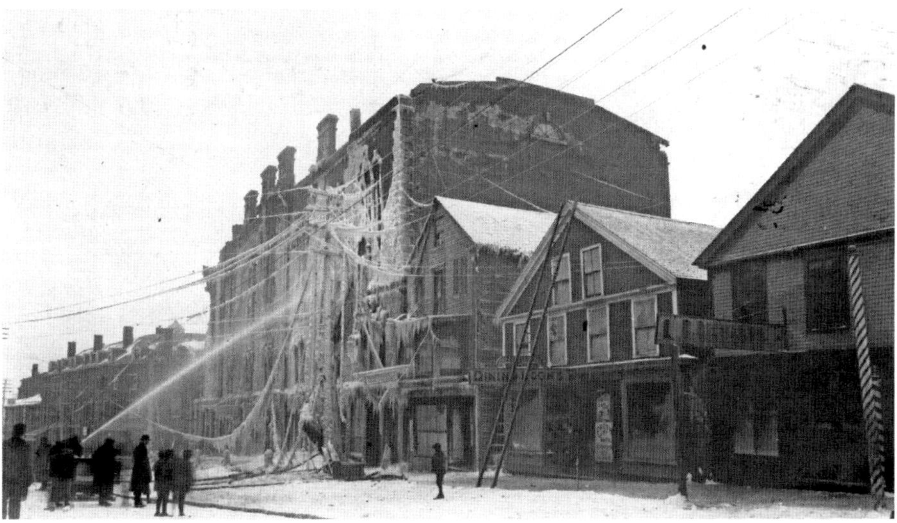

Above: The city found it difficult to fight fires in the nineteenth and early twentieth centuries, especially this one on December 30, 1894, which ruined the city building on Main Street. *McArthur Public Library Archive.*

Opposite, top: An unknown boy diving into the Saco River with Biddeford's skyline in the background, circa 1914. *Robert H. Gay Photograph Collection, courtesy of McArthur Public Library.*

Opposite, bottom: The circus's arrival in town was a popular event, especially the sight of an elephant, camel and other animals being marched down Main Street, as pictured here around 1905. *Robert H. Gay Photograph Collection, courtesy of McArthur Public Library.*

writer proffers, "the same story of gradual, but very evident diminution, has to be told."[120] The article continued to justify the actions of early settlers for the newly arrived masses, with little reprimand to those who displaced the local Sokoki tribe.

Advice columns were prominent features in newspapers throughout the latter part of the nineteenth century, especially ones that promoted proper manners and suggested suitable behavior for the young and vulnerable entering the adult world. On November 10, 1863, next to an advertisement for upcoming concerts at city hall, an article titled "How to Spend Evenings" provides appropriate examples, indicating first that "the character of many young men and women is decided for life by the way in which they spend their evenings."[121]

The writer continued: "An undue love for amusements in youth, and evenings given to self-indulgence, undermine strength of character, and unfit for success in the stern struggles of life." Youths who may have been reading this particular article were encouraged to spend evenings at home with their families, improving themselves through reading and study, or becoming involved with local religious groups.[122] The article, though dated in its tone, speaks to how times change, and its overall message remained the same for generations to come.

Part III

From Bustling to Bust

13

The Dawn of the Twentieth Century

By the turn of the twentieth century, Biddeford had become the urban hub of York County and was Maine's fourth-largest city. An electric railway provided transportation around downtown, electric lights illuminated the city streets, and city water and sewer systems were in place. Train service rolled through the city's downtown, allowing Biddeford to stay connected with larger hubs, including Portland to the north and Boston to the south. The city's "ethnic make up was diverse and urbane," with mainly English and French being spoken in the streets, but also German, Dutch, Albanian, Greek, Yiddish, Spanish, Chinese, Turkish, Danish, Polish, Russian and Italian. Living alongside the millworkers were business owners, doctors, lawyers, judges, druggists, opticians, superintendents, artisans and crafters.[123]

The hub that it was, Biddeford became a popular stop for travelers passing through and visitors who wished to stay a while. The city shops, theater acts, moving pictures and array of restaurants were busy with locals and city guests alike. One English visitor found great value in the price of a meal at many of Biddeford's restaurants. He remarked, "You may have as much as you please of everything for your quarter" at local restaurants. For just twenty-five cents, he reported you could feast on a hot dinner of "clam chowder, fried hornpout, macaroni and cheese, baked potatoes," with coffee, tea or milk. It also impressed this particular visitor that he could rent a six-room cottage for between four dollars and five dollars a month.[124]

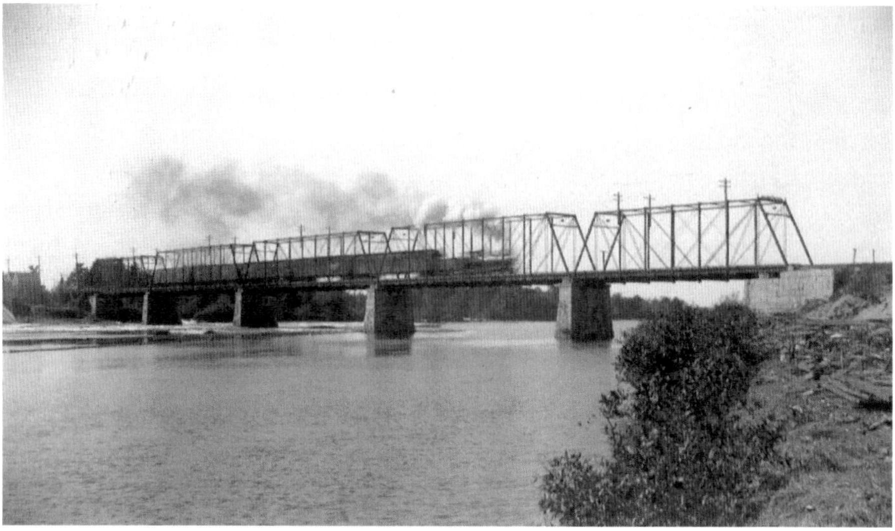

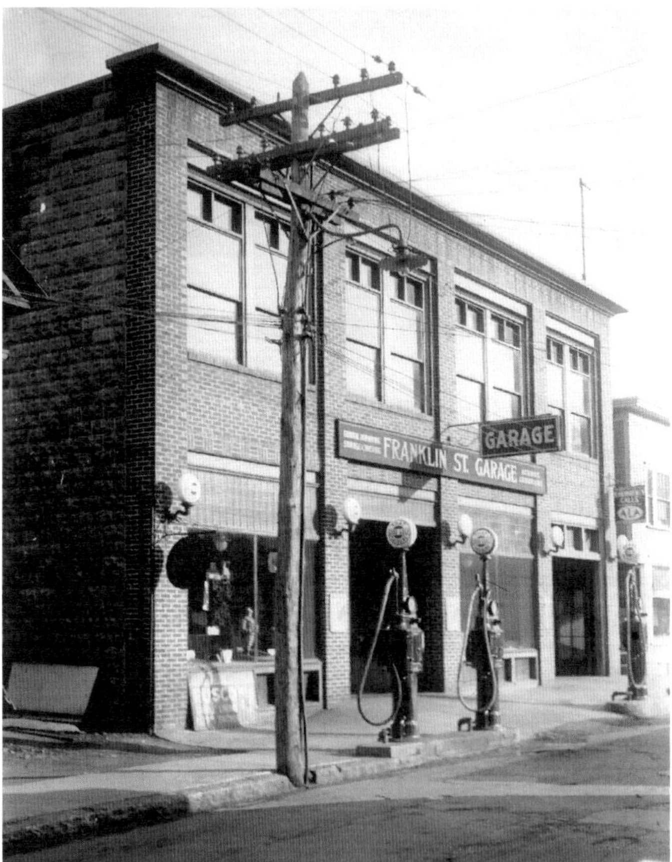

Above: A train crosses the Eastern Division bridge spanning the Saco River, circa 1890. *McArthur Public Library Archive.*

Left: Gas pumps outside a Franklin Street garage, circa 1919. *McArthur Public Library Archive.*

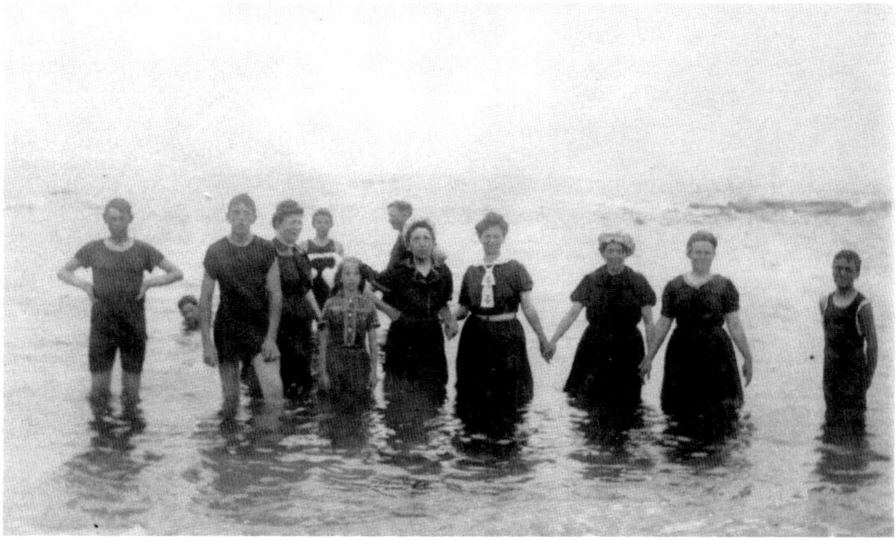

Biddeford's beaches were a popular destination for residents to enjoy a day of leisure. Pictured here is a group wading at Fortunes Rocks Beach, circa 1910. *McArthur Public Library Archive.*

Of course, with the ever-rising population of Biddeford and its surrounding towns, there was an increased need for medical care. Within the first decade of the twentieth century, the Trull Hospital and Webber Hospital were both founded. Trull, named for its founding doctor, was not only Biddeford's first hospital, but it was also the first homeopathic hospital in Maine. Webber, named for Pepperell Manufacturing Company's cloth room overseer Moses W. Webber, became the foundation on which York County's major hospital would grow over time.[125]

In addition to the bustling downtown, Biddeford's coastal community flourished. The region of Biddeford Pool, though inhabited first in the course of the city's history, was home to few families in the nineteenth century. One visitor estimated approximately seventy-five people called Biddeford Pool their home around 1840, but toward the end of the century, that number rose to more than two hundred people. "On pleasant days in the summer, a great many transient visitors came from Saco and Biddeford to spend the day and get a nice fish dinner," joining those who made Biddeford Pool their permanent residence or their annual vacation spot.[126]

In fact, this "down river resort" welcomed William H. Taft during his presidency. Leading up to Taft's visit, there was much speculation on when he would arrive, where he would stay and if residents would be able to meet

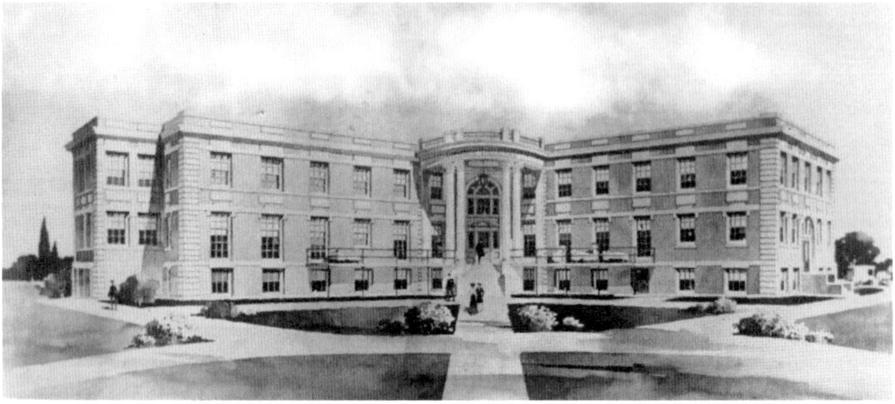

The Webber Hospital served the community until Southern Maine Medical Center was built. *McArthur Public Library Archive.*

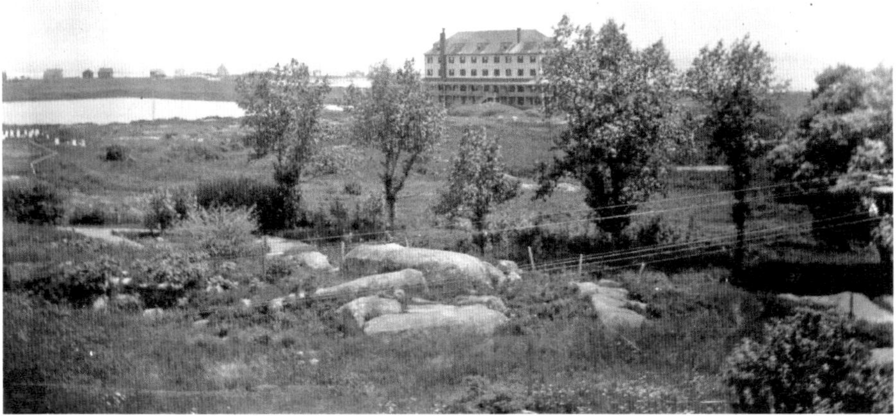

The Ocean View House, pictured in 1911, is now Marie Joseph Spiritual Center. It serves as a home to sisters of the Congregation of the Presentation of Mary and as a spiritual retreat for many. *Robert H. Gay Photograph Collection, courtesy of McArthur Public Library.*

Opposite, bottom: Many residents traveled to Biddeford Pool when word of President William Taft's visit circulated in the city. In this photo, Taft can be seen disembarking from his boat among a large crowd of onlookers. *McArthur Public Library Archive.*

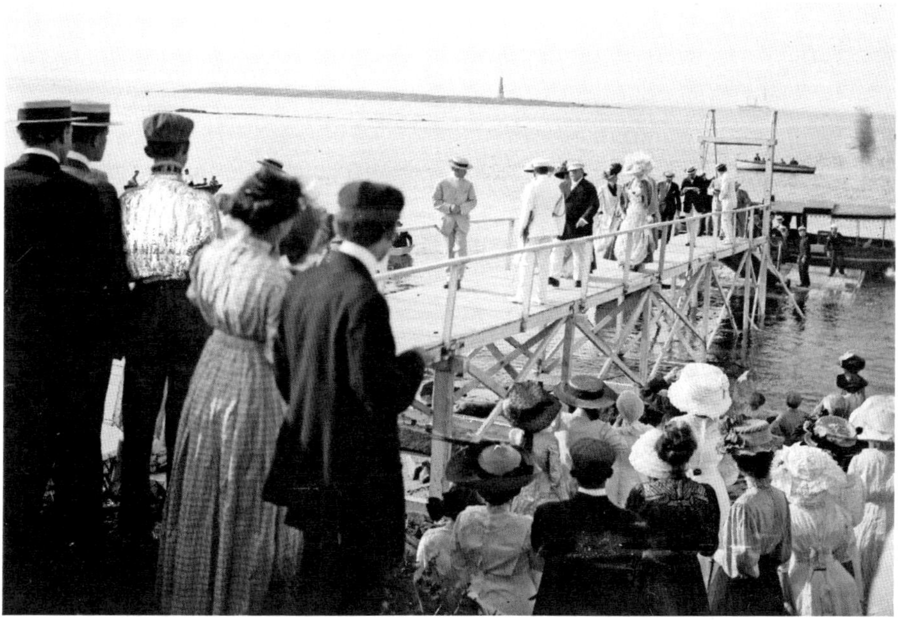

Locals await President William H. Taft's arrival in Biddeford Pool in July 1910, where he visited his sister-in-law, who was summering at a home along the golf course. *Robert H. Gay Photograph Collection, courtesy of McArthur Public Library.*

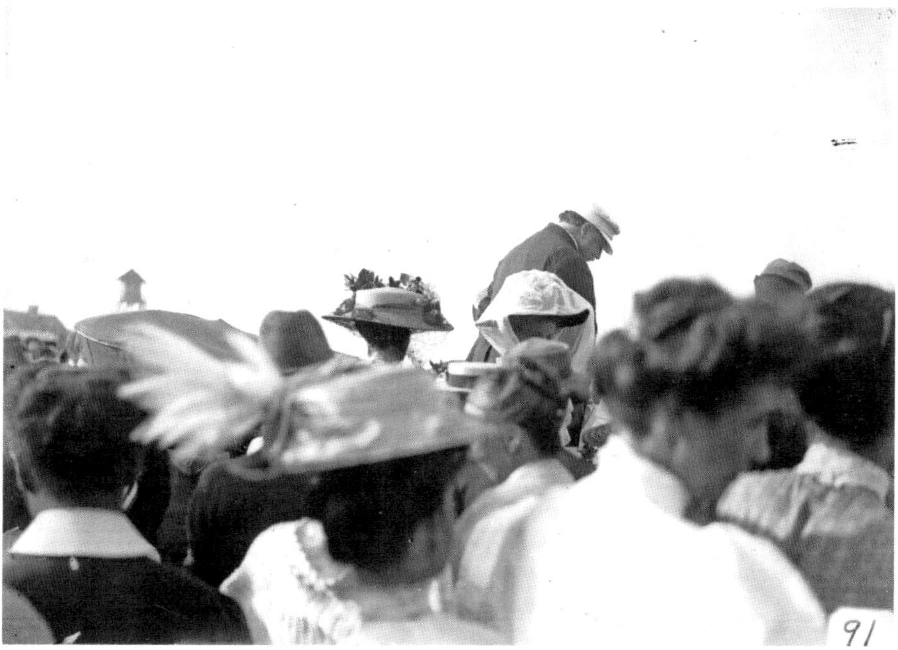

him. According to a newspaper article prior to his visit, "never before has the nation's chief executive paid the Pool the distinguished honor of a visit," though it was said to be a private, informal stop to visit his sister-in-law Louis T. Moore, who was summering near the golf course.[127] In preparation for Taft's visit, the community decorated their homes with bunting and American flags. On the day of his anticipated arrival, Biddeford residents traveled by ferry down the river or by automobile to Biddeford Pool to welcome him. It is rumored that Taft, known for his robust stature, nearly sank the float onto which he disembarked. However, while that story may not be true, the paper did report on the crowd that received America's twenty-seventh president before he was whisked off to his destination. "Throughout the distance, the crowds cheered and waved handkerchiefs and hats and in response to this greeting the President was kept busy uncovering his head, while the Taft smile was very much in evidence."[128]

With more than seventeen thousand residents in Biddeford, according to the 1910 U.S. census,[129] it is likely that a good portion of them witnessed Taft's arrival and departure that year, making his visit quite momentous for the city's coastal community. To date, Taft, George H.W. Bush and George W. Bush have been the only sitting presidents to visit Biddeford for pleasure.

Opposite: During Biddeford's Tercentenary Parade in 1916, local ladies participate in support of women's suffrage. *Robert H. Gay Photograph Collection, courtesy of McArthur Public Library.*

14

Amid the First World War

Biddeford celebrated its tercentennial and elected its first Franco-American mayor, Leopold A. Girard, in the midst of World War I. During the nineteen months the United States participated in the war, 825 Biddeford men joined the armed forces. Remarkably, only 31 of these men lost their lives in the line of duty.[130]

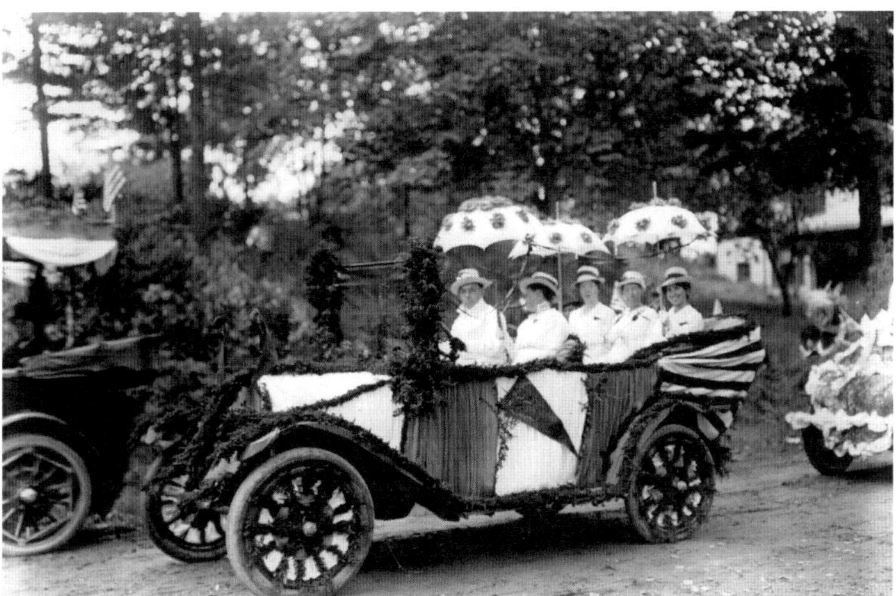

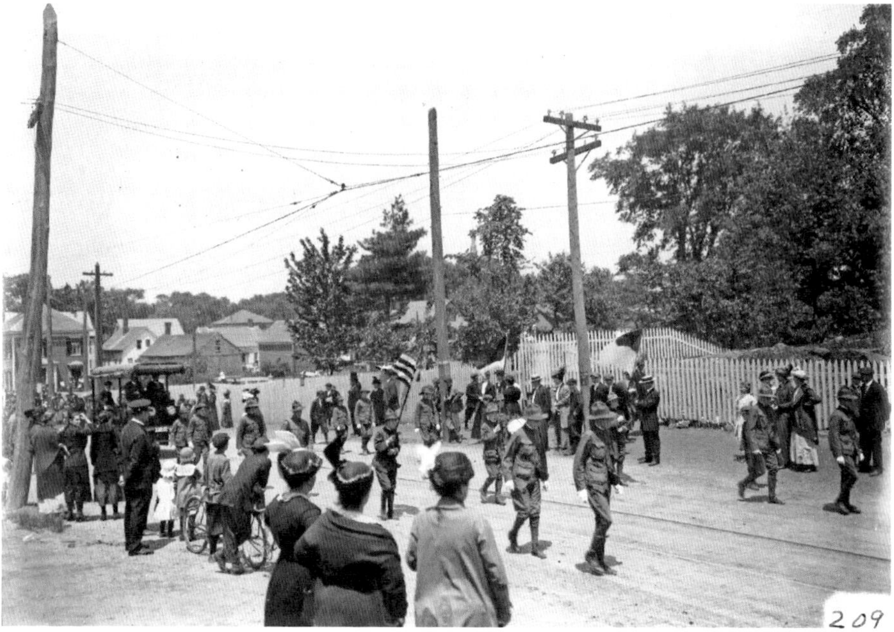

The Biddeford Boy Scouts participate in the city's tercentenary celebration parade, pictured on Birch Street near the intersection of Graham Street in 1916. *Robert H. Gay Photograph Collection, courtesy of McArthur Public Library.*

The *Biddeford Daily Journal* and the *Weekly Record* included national news, war developments and even occasional photos of soldiers in combat. However, the daily happenings around town remained much unchanged. On Adams Street, residents frequented the Nickel, "the most up to date moving picture house" around.[131] The movies shown at the Nickel began to rival performances at the nearby Opera House. At Central Theater, ten cents would buy admission for three vaudeville acts.[132] These theaters provided entertainment for residents and an escape from the daily drudgery of life and news of the war.

As during the Civil War, Pepperell Manufacturing Company stayed busy "furnishing millions of yards of cloth for Army khaki and Navy white" uniforms. Saco & Lowell Machine Shop maintained its production as well, providing parts for various war mechanisms.[133] The addition of Sears Roebuck Shoe Shop in Biddeford also helped to meet the demand of military footwear; it also put pressure on neighboring Saco to add more housing for the shop's employees. In fact, three flat apartment houses were anticipated for the summer of 1917.[134] The wartime demand also caused

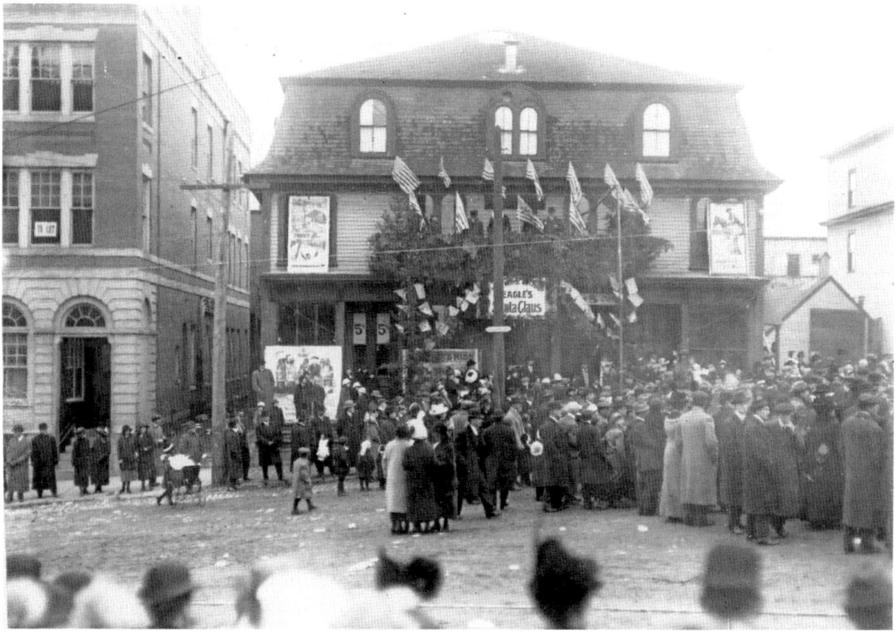

Crowds watch the distribution of 2,500 boxes of candy in front of the Nickel Theater on Christmas morning 1913. *McArthur Public Library Archive.*

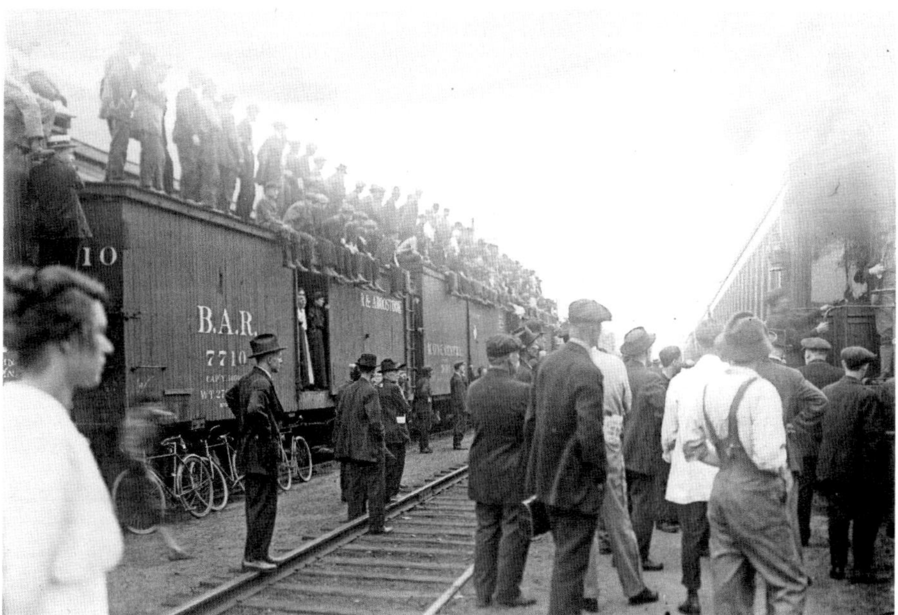

The Seventh Company, U.S. Army Coast Artillery Corps, departing by rail in 1917. *Robert H. Gay Photograph Collection, courtesy of McArthur Public Library.*

a revival of shipbuilding on the Saco River: "A company was formed, the ancient Perkins' shipyard on the riverbank below the Main Street bridge was re-equipped, and a large four-mast schooner built."[135] The *Jere G. Shaw* ended up being the last vessel of its size—193 feet long by 36 feet wide—to be built in Biddeford of local oak.[136]

While the wartime effort kept Biddeford's economy bustling, cultural tensions in this melting pot of a community were still quite high, especially toward the Franco-American workers. In March 1917, a group of Pepperell Manufacturing Company weavers walked out and went on strike. While they returned a few days later, it was claimed that "some of the men who came out on the strike and are believed to be at the bottom of the walkout have made the statement to the French weavers that they would "fix" them if they did not stay out until the strike was settled to their satisfaction."[137] This "nativist hatred" rose not only in Biddeford, but across the state as well, after World War I ended. This nativism drove the reformation of the Ku Klux Klan, which gathered some forty thousand members statewide, including

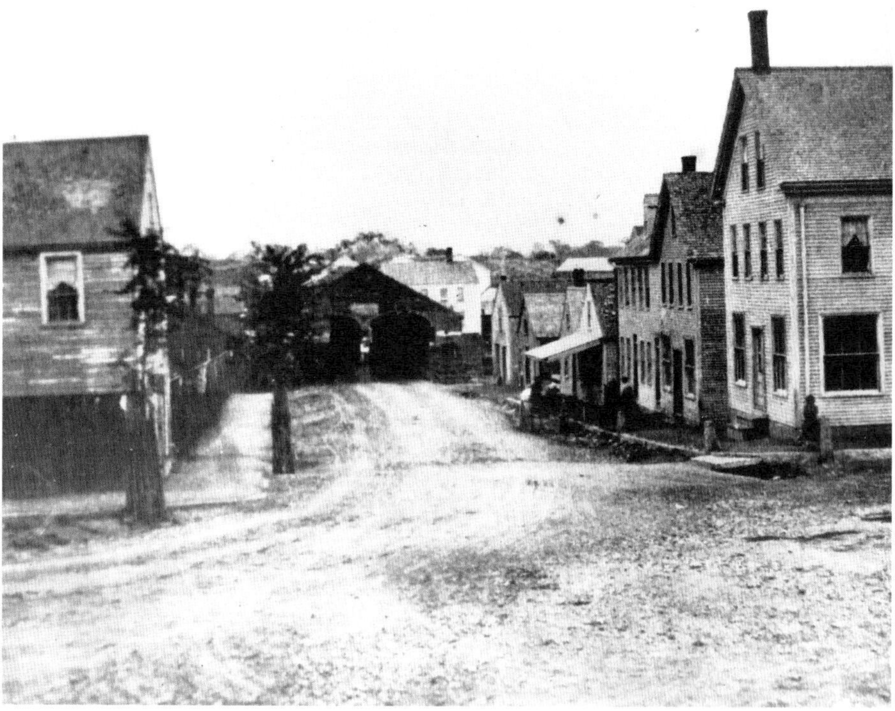

A covered bridge connecting the Main Streets of Biddeford and Saco. It was torn down in 1877. *McArthur Public Library Archive.*

doctors, lawyers, businesspeople, ministers and farmers.[138] This "secret, fraternal society" was fueled by anxiety about the economy, the Russian Revolution and raids on union leaders, and its members placed blame on low-class and ethnic citizens for job losses and societal changes.[139]

According to local legend, the Ku Klux Klan targeted the Franco-Americans of Biddeford. It is said that "the Klan paraded through Saco and tried to come to Biddeford. The story goes that the Irish blocked the Bradbury Street Bridge and the French blocked the Main Street Bridge. Both groups were well-armed and ready to chase the scoundrels back to Saco at any cost."[140] It is believed that the crowd of angry French and Irish Catholics was enough to scare the Klan into retreat. While it is possible this attempted attack by the Ku Klux Klan may be folklore, there is a noticeable shift in Biddeford's cultural climate after the mid-1920s. Immigrant groups hailing from various countries began to mingle more, cultural traditions started to blend and the relationships between white, Protestant descendants of early settlers and those who were deemed "newcomers" began to stabilize.

15
A Country United

On December 7, 1941, the Japanese air force bombed Pearl Harbor, Hawaii, dragging America into World War II. Though the ongoing war spurred fear among Americans, the country's sudden involvement united neighbors and prompted action locally. Shortly after the bombing, the *Biddeford Daily Journal* replaced birth announcements with photos of men enlisting in the armed forces. Marriage announcements became more prevalent as neighborhood sweethearts pledged their love for each other prior to being separated by military service.

The demand for military supplies was once again the focus of Biddeford's mills. In a regular newspaper column titled "This Week at Pepperell," it was reported:

> *Textiles are important to America's present crisis. In fact, so important that some of the cloth woven by Pepperell was given one of the first government priorities in textile manufacturing. They are used in finishing some of the most important machine parts on planes, ships, tanks, guns, machine tools and other major parts that are important in defending our freedom.*[141]

The city's mills recruited heavily for anyone not drafted or enlisting with a branch of the military. The workforce needed to be maintained in order to meet the constant demand for war goods.

Opposite, bottom: An unknown artist's pen-and-ink sketch of the Saco-Lowell Shops as seen from Elm Street, circa 1948. *McArthur Public Library Archive*.

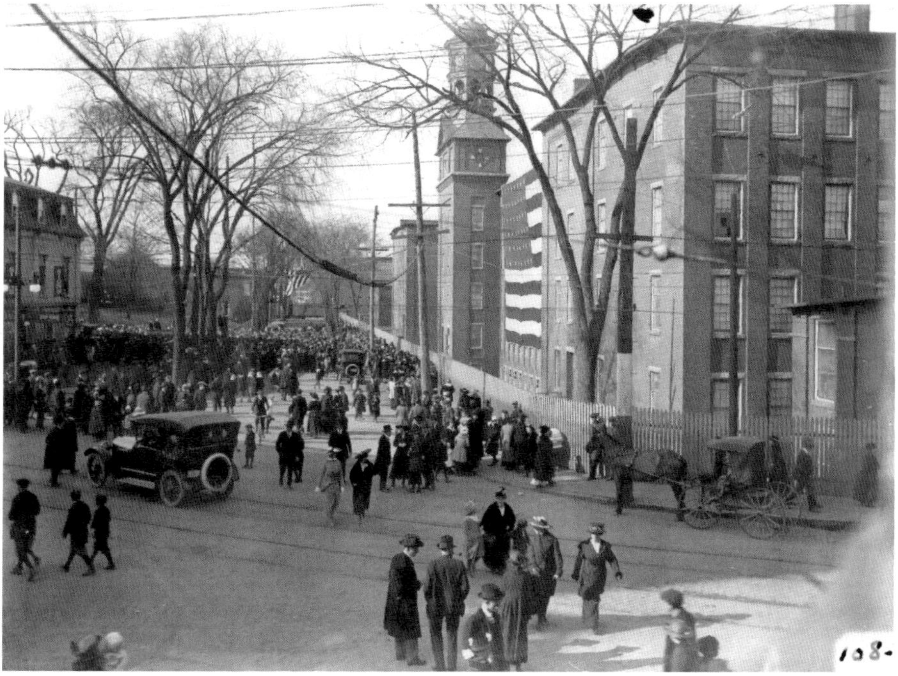

In the midst of World War I, on April 14, 1917, a three-hundred-pound American flag on loan from Filene's of Boston was hung at Pepperell Manufacturing Company's Mill No. 3 on Lincoln Street. *Robert H. Gay Photograph Collection, courtesy of McArthur Public Library.*

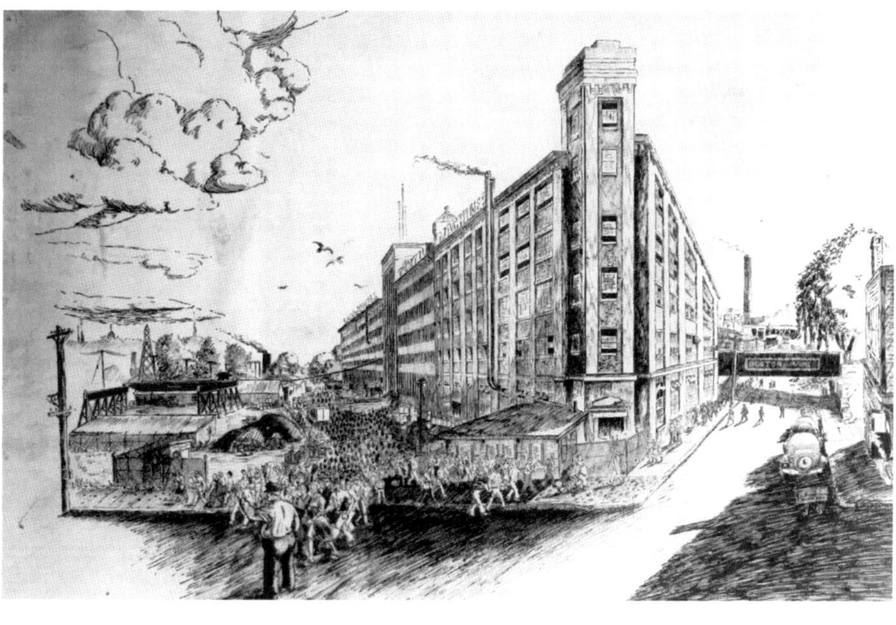

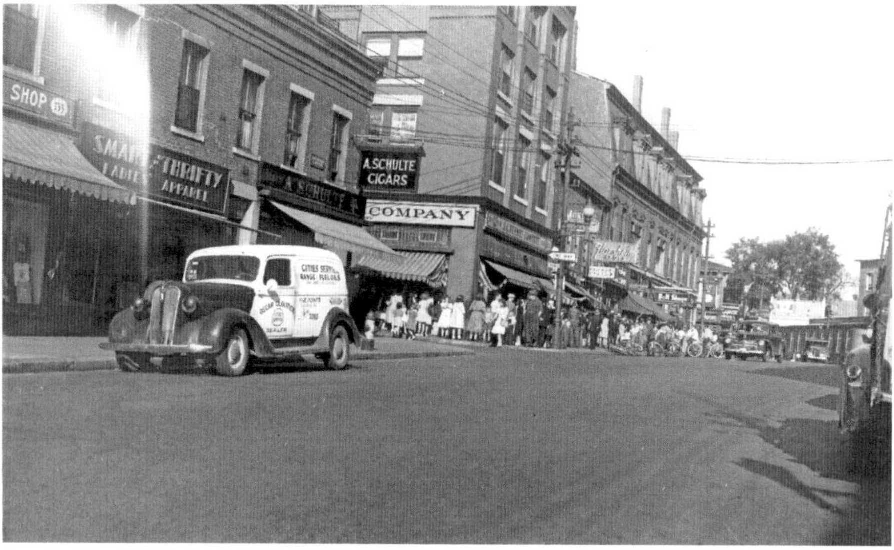

Residents standing in the butter line on Main Street during the rationing of World War II, circa 1943. *McArthur Public Library Archive.*

Amid newspaper columns of social items and personal briefs, pictures of local men in the service were featured with short items about their participation in the war. On a weekly basis, the *Biddeford Daily Journal* listed a ration timetable with the "Home Front Pledge," which stated, "I will pay no more than top legal prices. I will accept no rationed goods without giving up rationed stamps."[142] Rationed items varied, but for the first week of September 1943, sugar, shoes, tire inspections, gasoline and the use of wood, coal, gas or oil for heating and cooking were rationed. Additionally, residents were encouraged to participate in war loan drives to "back the invasion" and support the military.[143]

The ongoing war effort united those who remained stateside. Their daily work in the mills was important and together they took pride in playing even a small part in the war effort. Those at home received letters from their loved ones at war. Though stateside relatives often had no idea where these men were, some active duty members found ways to convey their location through coded letters. Roland Bouthillette enlisted in the U.S. Navy and served in the South Pacific during World War II. He was a cook for the crew on the USS *Clay*. Early in his appointment, Bouthillette wrote to his new wife, Gisele, providing her clues to his whereabouts.[144] If he used his name, it meant he was on base in Honolulu, Hawaii, but "Ronald" indicated China, "Laura" indicated Portugal and "Lionel"

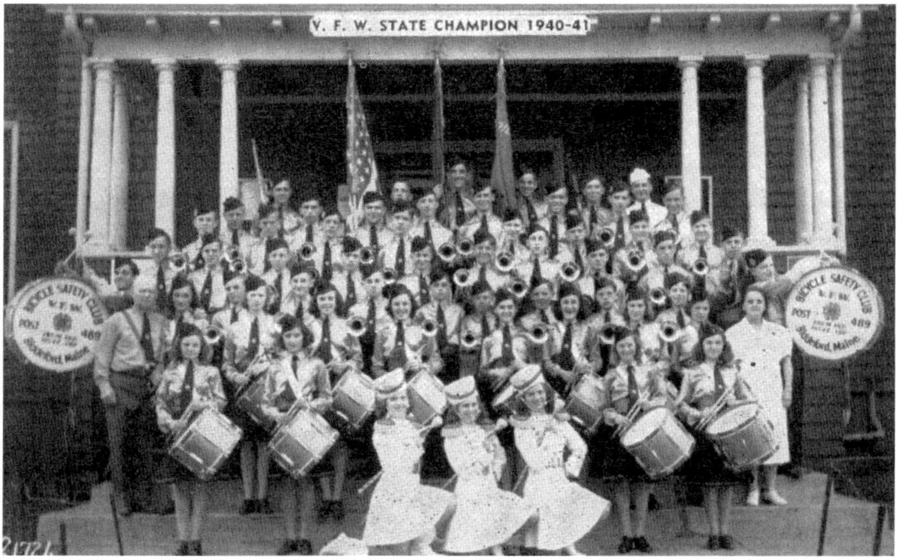

VFW Bicycle Safety Club, Drum and Bugle Corps, Post 489, during its first public appearance, May 30, 1940. *Richard N. Carr Collection, courtesy of McArthur Public Library.*

meant South America. This allowed his family to know where his ship had been or where it was headed.

The letters from loved ones brought little comfort when paired with the harrowing headlines. However, residents tried to find enjoyment in day-to-day life. Shops downtown continued to advertise, but with a savvy shopper in mind. Youland's, a small jewelry dealer, enticed ladies with "exciting jewelry" for one dollar and up. Butlers, a popular department store on Main Street, boasted back-to-school footwear, blanket sales and "sport clothes." It suggested to readers, "Build your wardrobe around sports clothes, wonderful for school, work, for USO fun!"[145]

Even with many men serving their country, Biddeford residents could not deny their excitement for another season of high school football. Biddeford High School athletic director Steve White was proud to announce that, "unlike some schools, Biddeford has anticipated a full schedule of games for the coming fall, with the usual Sanford and Thornton games the highlights of the season."[146] This particular year, the rivalry games were held on Biddeford's turf. This was cause for extra enthusiasm around the Thornton game, a rivalry that started in 1893 and continues in school sports today.

16

Midcentury Shift

The spring of 1947 came quickly for Maine, melting the state's snowpack and warming the region for summer. The mild weather was welcomed, but unprecedented. Then, in mid-July, a stretch of rain-free weather began that would last through October. With a booming tourist industry, no one could complain about the fair weather, but when drought became a major concern, residents were put on alert due to a "high state of inflammability." In the first week of October, a single forest fire was spotted, then a second and a third. Within two weeks, twenty separate fires were burning, blanketing the state in smoke and ash.[147]

Downtown Biddeford was mostly spared, but the coastal community met a different fate. A line of blazes threatening Trull and Webber Hospitals drew the firefighting force away from the coast, but an "unexpected shift in wind" destroyed all but 6 cottages in the coastal area known as Fortunes Rocks.[148] The cottages destroyed were among the 397 seasonal and 851 year-round homes destroyed by some two hundred fires that ravaged the state. Nearly a quarter of a million acres of forest was consumed, and nine towns burned to the ground, costing York County alone some $3 million in damages.[149]

Those who lived through the menacing fires still recall the scene.

> *The thickness of the smoke which obscured the sun and sky, the roaring sound of an approaching wall of flame and the lingering smell of charred woods and homes...some who fought the fire are reluctant to relive it,*

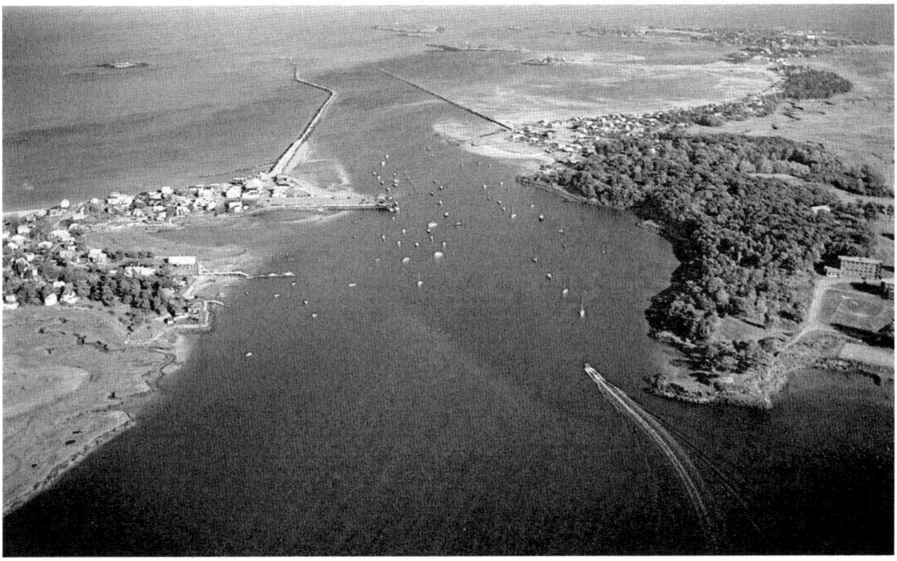

A 1988 aerial view of the Saco Bay, including Camp Ellis, Hills Beach, Biddeford Pool and Fletcher's Neck, where the Saco River flows into the Atlantic Ocean. *Richard N. Carr Collection, courtesy of McArthur Public Library.*

> *recalling how they faced the flames with minimal equipment, their eyes and throats burning, feet hot, having had no sleep and little to eat or drink.*[150]

The only thing that seemed to stop the fire from progressing eastward was the Atlantic Ocean.

While the center of Biddeford remained mostly intact after the fires, this major moment in Maine's history seemed to also mark a shift in industry in the city. In 1916, Pepperell Manufacturing Company had its best year with 74.8 million yards of cotton sold. Since then, demand had decreased and production was down, as were profits. In the 1930s, the company built a new plant in Alabama, closer to the sources of its cotton. Over the next twenty years, the majority of operations had moved south. Biddeford was left with only about fifteen hundred jobs to fill.[151]

This exodus of jobs impacted the city greatly. Residents formerly gainfully employed could not find work, and some were forced to move for jobs. Others sought work outside the city, and Main Street no longer saw the foot traffic it once did when millworkers flooded the streets between shifts and on lunch breaks. In the city's 1956 annual report, Mayor Albert Lambert said:

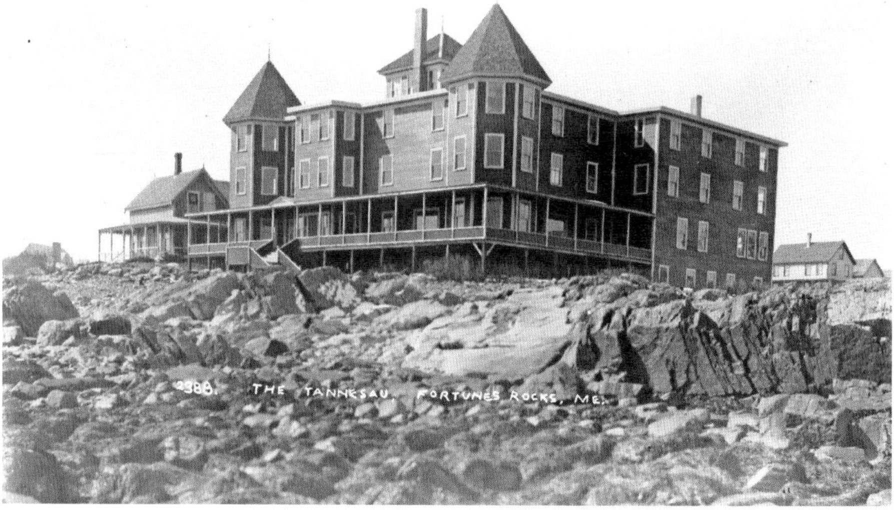

A view of Hotel Tannesau on Fortunes Rocks Beach, circa 1909. *McArthur Public Library Archive.*

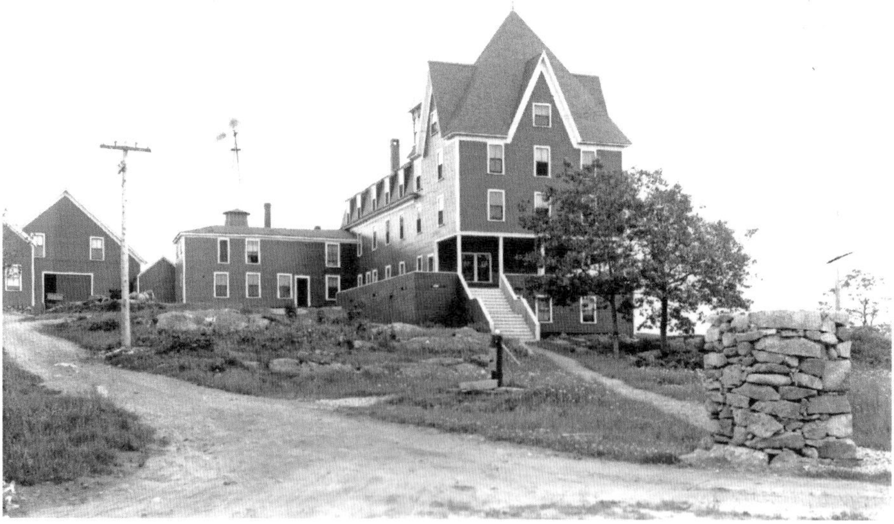

Hotel Rox, as seen here from the road, was another spot for summer people to stay and enjoy Biddeford's beaches. *Robert H. Gay Photograph Collection, courtesy of McArthur Public Library.*

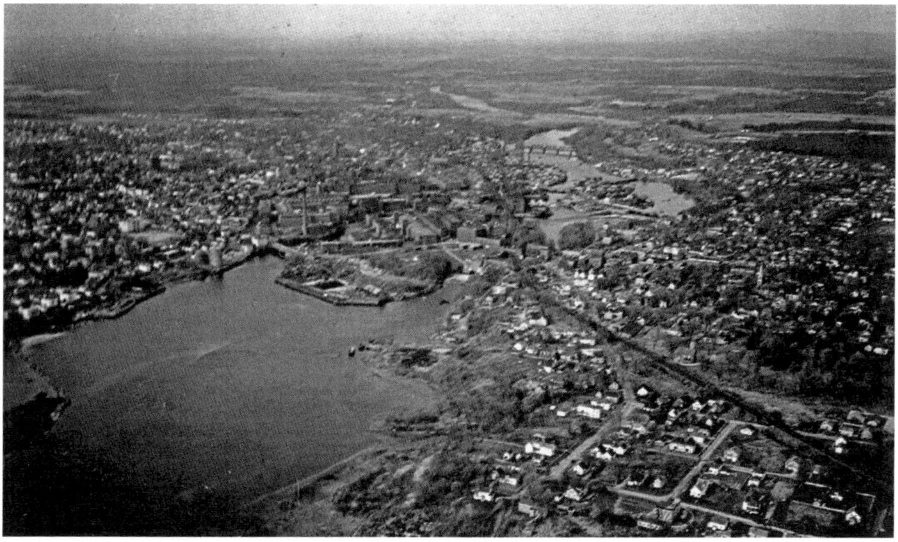

An aerial view of Biddeford's downtown, circa 1950. *Richard N. Carr Collection, courtesy of McArthur Public Library.*

> *We have been fortunate in having in Biddeford a variety of skilled labor, from heavy machinery operations to textile and shoe workers. Some of these workers have moved to other sections in the country. They now live in communities that, in the past, had the foresight to encourage new industry. Our commission must now surpass the efforts of other, more progressive communities.*[152]

In the same report, Mayor Lambert suggested the city survey its citizens to know where they work and where they shop. If residents were not shopping in Biddeford, he suggested the city and merchants investigate how to "regain the support" of local shoppers.

However, two years later, the outlook remained bleak. Mayor Clement Deschambeault wrote in the 1958 annual report that "many have faced the hardships of unemployment, of trying to make ends meet on a limited budget, of struggling to meet steadily rising costs on dwindling incomes."[153] The city's welfare department had seen an increased demand, with a $25,000 increase in department spending over the course of the year. The jump in budget was due to the fact that only 962 people received benefits in 1957; that number rose drastically to 3,712 the following year.[154]

In April 1963, another historic fire threatened the infrastructure of the city and destroyed a half-square mile of land downtown. The blaze was

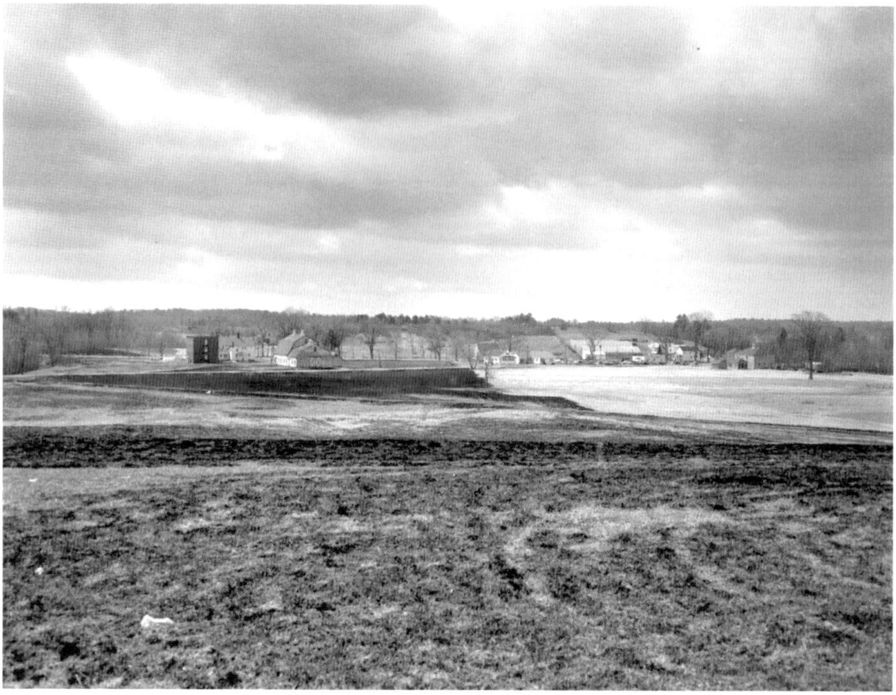

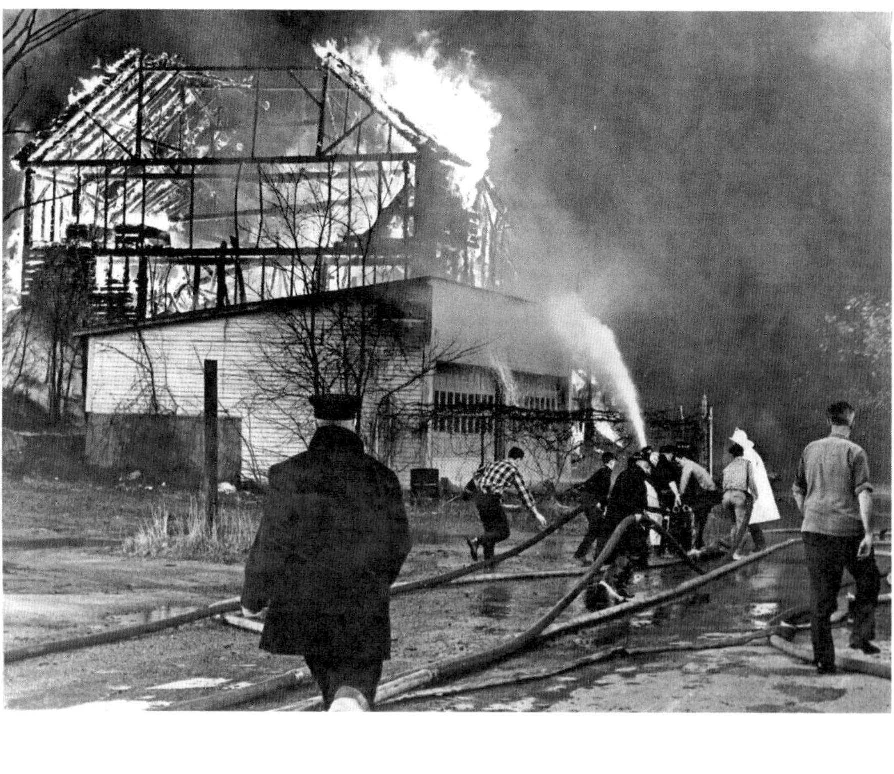

sparked in the Diamond National lumberyard; "the wood of the lumberyard fed the fire so well that the intense heat scorched thousands of feet of fire hose."[155] The wind carried the fire across to Hooper Street, destroying fifteen homes and the lumberyard, despite the full-force response of 300 firemen from thirteen communities. This immense fire left 142 people homeless and a company in ruins, yet city officials remained hopeful that Biddeford's manufacturing industry could rebound from its surmounting troubles.

Opposite, top: Biddeford City Poor Farm near South and Main Streets, circa 1950. *McArthur Public Library Archive.*

Opposite, bottom: Firefighters and volunteers battle the blaze during the Diamond National/ Hooper Street fire on April 20, 1963. *McArthur Public Library Archive.*

17
OUTSOURCING

In 1968, Pepperell Manufacturing Company merged with WestPoint Georgia, becoming WestPoint Pepperell. This corporate move was the first of many to come over the next fifty years. At the time, employees remained hopeful that the merger would mean a resurgence of jobs. However, "urged on by the anorexic vision that you can never be too thin, streamlined companies [including textile mills] may have their design, research, manufacturing, shipping, advertising, billing, paying and collecting all done out of house."[156] The age of outsourcing had arrived, and WestPoint Pepperell was not immune to this lean business model.

According to Mike Cavanaugh, the local director of Union of Needletrades Industrial Textile Employees at the time, New England mills were bracing for the worst while hoping for the best. He said:

> *The mood was, whichever way it goes* [move out entirely or keep some work in Biddeford], *we got to be prepared to deal with a lot of unemployed people. In the meantime, what kind of package* [tax breaks, wage cuts, etc.] *can we put together to make ourselves the most attractive to cooperation…if we sit in a corner, make ourselves as small as possible, breath very little air, maybe someone wouldn't mind letting us survive.*[157]

Rene Boisvert, vice president and general manager of the remaining mills, saw a different approach by distinguishing the Biddeford division. "The talents of the people, the work ethic of the people, are so important,

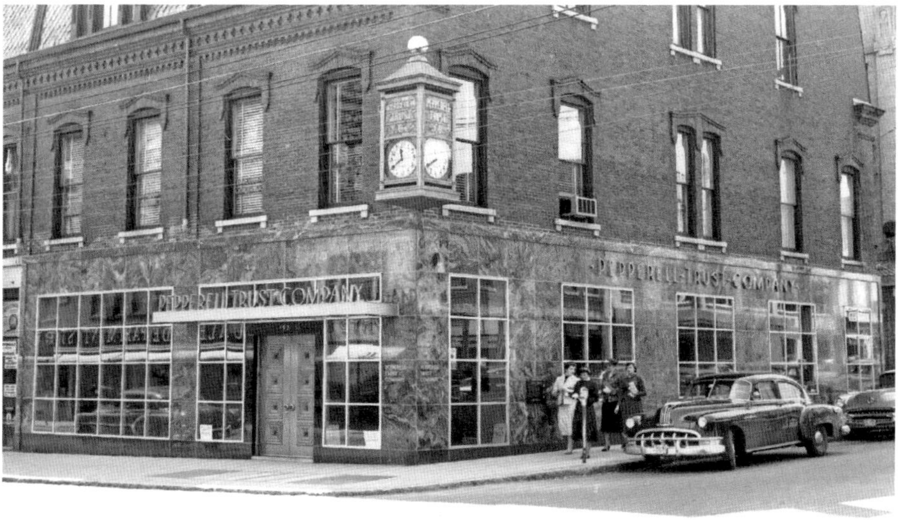

The Pepperell Trust Company on Main Street, circa 1955. *McArthur Public Library Archive.*

but what keeps them on their job is modernization," and so he led the charge to invest $10.8 million to bring the old mills up to date. In 1988, Boisvert said, "We replaced ninety percent or more of our old equipment in the past ten years with the latest, state-of-the-art technology in textile machinery."[158] While investing in the mill, he also worked to keep labor costs down and people employed.

Over the course of Pepperell Manufacturing Company's history, including its various mergers, sales and company changes, the end goal shifted. Francis Skinner's ideal of focusing on outstanding quality was replaced by a demand for quantity with growing sales margins. It was also no longer a company centered in Biddeford. While Boisvert had a vested interest in taking care of mill employees, the company was solely focused on numbers—production and profits. His efforts to prove Biddeford's mills were worth the money and attention—and employees worth their paychecks—were continually undermined by corporate maneuvers.

In 1971, WestPoint Pepperell sold its blanket division to Sunbeam. Biddeford's millworkers were now responsible for making the blanket shells for the corporation's electric blankets.[159] By 1978, Biddeford workers were again on the picket line, staging a nine-week strike for better wages and working conditions. This was not the first strike seen by Biddeford mills, and the demands of the walkout were not different from those made by

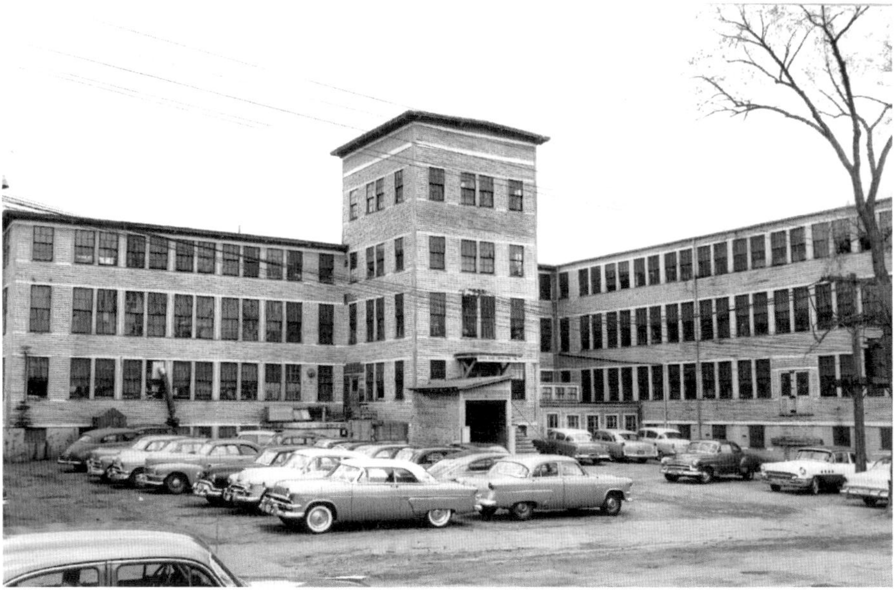

The home of Bruce Shoe Company and Mitchell Shoe Company, circa 1955. *McArthur Public Library Archive.*

employees in the 1800s. However, the corporate investors were not as responsive as early mill agents, because, ultimately, "keeping the mill open in Biddeford [was] not a legitimate use of investors' money, nor [was] making good blankets."[160]

Work would continue to be sent elsewhere, and jobs would slowly trickle to other parts of the country over the next two decades. Biddeford, however, was not alone in losing valuable employment opportunities. According to the country's Bureau of Labor Statistics, "about ten times a week, a big factory shuts down somewhere in the United States, throwing an average of 190 people out of work."[161] By 1997, the remaining millwork in the city employed only about 300 people and "few jobs in the local market come close to the $9 to $13 an hour workers are paid to tend the thrumming weaving machines."[162] According to local resident and historian Charles Butler Jr., mill jobs are "the cream. Jobs pass down in families from one generation to the next because of the wages and health benefits are good compared to anything else available in town."[163] Yet "mill hands [continue to] rely on a tradition of grit to see them through hard times."[164]

18

Searching for Something

In 1982, as Biddeford's economy struggled, Joseph Plamondon founded a cultural festival to celebrate the still-thriving Franco-American community in the city. La Kermesse would grow to become a popular weekend-long event held toward the end of June, during which families would enjoy Franco-American cuisine, music, dance and other fairground favorites.[165] While the intention to unite a community struggling with the changed economy in Biddeford's downtown was a success, the singular event was not enough to generate business downtown.

Many of the mill buildings were now vacant, with only a fraction of the factory space still in use for the remaining production of blankets. City officials could clearly see that the manufacturing industry was nearing its long, drawn-out death. Residents were seeking jobs outside the city, and local stores struggled to compete with supermarkets and box chains that opened at the Maine Mall. The city's economy floundered, and officials scrambled for a solution to rescue it from the downward spiral it had been experiencing for years.

At first, officials tossed around the idea of generating steam power to feed into the electricity grid. Concurrently, officials also needed to mitigate the environmental hazards of the leaking landfills and find a new means of disposing of city waste. Early discussions between the twin cities led Biddeford and Saco to propose a trash-to-energy plant, which would eliminate the need for landfills, allow both cities to be rid of trash for relatively low fees and produce energy through the burning of trash. The cities signed a contract in

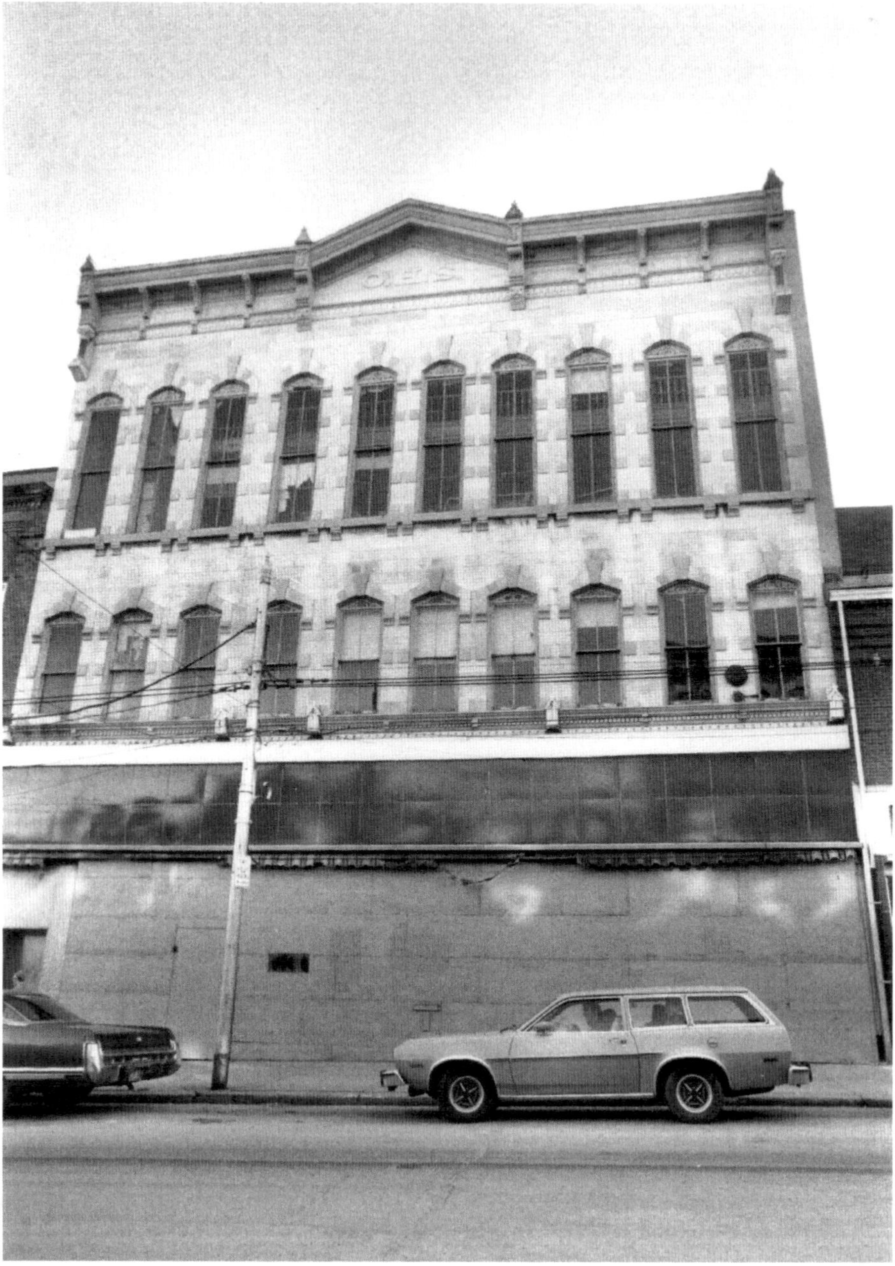

The prominent O.H. Staples Block on Main Street. *McArthur Public Library Archive.*

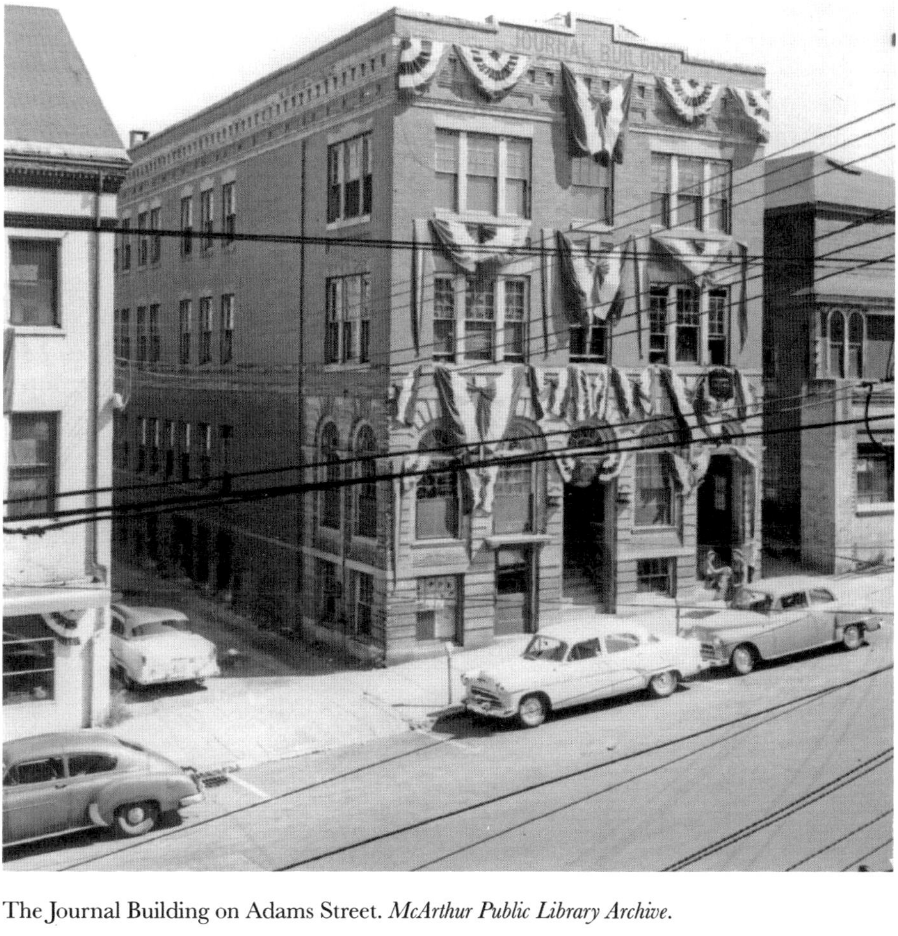

The Journal Building on Adams Street. *McArthur Public Library Archive.*

1983 with Kuhr Technologies Inc. and General Electric with plans to build Maine Energy Recovery Company, a trash incinerator that would generate power to feed the Central Maine Power grid.[166]

The nature of the incinerator required it to be located near a water source to help cool the facility after trash was burned. It also needed to be in proximity to a substation for the purpose of feeding power into the grid. This led Saco and Biddeford to identify four potential locations: in Biddeford's industrial park off Route 111, in Saco's industrial park off North Street, on Saco's Factory Island and at a defunct factory site off Lincoln Street in Biddeford.[167] Maine Energy Recover Company opted for the old factory site, paying $758,000 for six and a half acres along the Saco River.[168]

In the fall of 1986, testing of Maine Energy Recover's massive plant took place. The $106 million downtown incinerator was on target to complete construction by the spring of 1987, but the testing was seen as a "training exercise for our people and a way to give us a realistic view of how the equipment is going to work," according to Maine Energy Recover Company project manager E. Peter Brown.[169] He believed "the start up would allow officials to check the equipment and gauge things like traffic flow," which would add sixty to seventy container trucks rolling through Biddeford's downtown.[170] During the construction process, residents started to voice concern over the plant's location, but a petition of eight hundred signatures was deemed to have come "too late" to consider changing plans.[171]

At the time, Board of Environmental Protection chairman Samuel Zaitlin touted "Maine Energy Recovery Co. as the wave of the future for Maine and the nation."[172] However, this notion would be dismissed not long after the incinerator opened for business in April 1987. Complaints came pouring in to city officials regarding the smell, the appearance, the noise and the general dissatisfaction with the plant's operations. In a letter to the editor published on August 25, 1988, resident and downtown business owner Dana Perkins wrote:

> *Very simply, the smell is awful. When the wind is right, I smell it up at my house* [on Elm Street], *and at its worst, it has awakened us in the middle of the night. The drone of the plant and the beep beeping of the trucks can be heard up there at times too. Going past the plant is a lot more grim.*[173]

Within a year, it was rumored that the employees at the plant would walk out because "operators of Maine Energy Recovery Co. can't meet guidelines for health and safety."[174] Employees reported "confusion of upper management about how to run the plant and fear among employees of dangerous working conditions."[175] Within two years of the plant's opening, Zaitlin admitted, "if we knew then what we know now, several things would have been done differently."[176] Biddeford Community Development director Robert Dodge concurred: "It doesn't take a PhD in land use planning to recognize the location of the plant was a mistake."[177]

Among the complaints, accusations were being made about how the location was picked. However, it "appears [the location decision was] based on outdated assumptions about the character of downtown, financial expectations that never panned out, and the lack of significant opposition early on."[178] Unfortunately, the late opposition and worries expressed by residents had little impact once the plant was in operation. The downtown trash incinerator would be a point of contention for nearly thirty years, often pitting officials and residents of Saco and Biddeford against each other.

19

Trash Town, U.S.A.

Within the last decade of the twentieth century, Biddeford struggled to escape the issues brought on by Maine Energy Recovery Company. The stench from the incinerator was pervasive. The plant could not adequately keep pace with incoming trash. Trash trucks snarled traffic on Main and Elm Streets and added to the wear and tear on the roads. "The people who [were] proud of their city [became] horrified that a project of this magnitude could be put in this location and effect so many." Biddeford came to be known as "Trash Town, U.S.A."[179]

Biddeford loomed under the shadow of the abandoned mill buildings. What remained in operation only occupied a fraction of the hundreds of thousands of square feet in the mill buildings downtown. A last-ditch effort to save the industry happened in 1997, when a group of employees and investors bought out Sunbeam-Oster with a five-year agreement. Biddeford Textile would claim bankruptcy within four years' time.

Stores like Butler's, Woolworth's and Fisherman's could no longer compete with the variety offered by nationwide chains at the mall and the discounts available at Walmart, which opened in 1995 just off the highway exit for Biddeford. The Main Street that was once "so crowded that you couldn't even walk on the sidewalks on a Saturday night" was now desolate; Renee O'Neill, former business manager of the City Theater, said, "It wasn't just that, [but rather] what happens downtown is pretty much fueled by the people who live and work downtown.[180] A mill workforce that was once numbered in the few thousands was now only a few hundred.

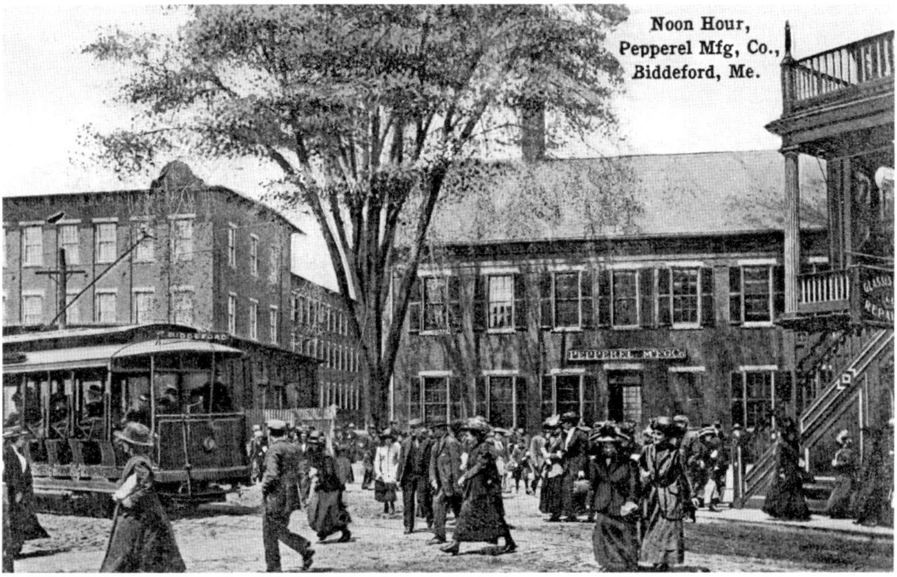

A postcard of the noontime lunch hour, when Pepperell Manufacturing Company employees would flood the streets during their break, circa 1916. *Richard N. Carr Collection, courtesy of McArthur Public Library.*

With others commuting for work, there was no reason for them to visit downtown. Most storefronts were dark by 5:00 p.m., and restaurants could no longer survive.

Meanwhile, the tipping fees the city planned on saving by having a trash incinerator downtown was not nearly enough to help the city's budget. Between the loss of business downtown and increasing costs, the city was forced to pass the price on to residents. Property taxes increased dramatically, and nearly 30 percent of this burden fell to coastal residents with high property assessments on mostly seasonal homes. By the late 1990s, residents of Biddeford Pool attempted to secede from Biddeford and develop their own government. The secession was led in part by retired four-star general Wallace Nutting. He explained that, in addition to the tax burden, residents felt removed from the city. He said, "in recent years, regular folks [as opposed to 'wealthy summer people'] have tried to live at the beaches year-round and there has been a conscious effort to recognize that we're all one community."[181] While the secession ultimately failed, the discord was pervasive, and the city made little effort to define a sense of community within the city.

Local politics did not do any favors for Biddeford's diminishing persona. The political scene was described as colorful, divisive and dysfunctional:

"Flaws in the city charter, such as liberal mayoral power and partisan primaries to nominate candidates were exposed."[182] It came to light that former mayor Robert Farley overruled the city's zoning board denials and approved construction for Maine Energy Recovery Company despite alternate recommendations. By the turn of the twenty-first century, the incinerator had become widely considered the primary obstacle to the city's redevelopment. Add to that adverse decisions made by Mayor James Grattelo, including a veto of teachers' pay raises in 1995 that led to lengthy legal proceedings, staff resignations and firings of city administration.[183]

A city that once attracted thousands of French-Canadian immigrants to live and work was now considered an urban desert with no available jobs. It was no longer favorable to call home. City officials were now revisiting ideas set forth some fifty years earlier, when Mayor Albert Lambert[184] sought to attract a new industry to the area to bring job opportunities back into the community. Only this time, the focus was less on developing an industrial park and more on what to do with all those vacant mill buildings.

Part IV

Reimagining, Rehabilitating, Revitalizing

20
Finding the Heart in Biddeford

In need of change, Biddeford found it in the form of Wallace Nutting, a retired U.S. Army four-star general. With less than three months to the November 2003 mayoral election, Nutting added his name to the ballot. Many thought Nutting's bid for mayor was a longshot. The city traditionally voted Democrat, and the general was a Republican. Biddeford's football rivalry with Saco spilled over into many other arenas, politics included, and Nutting, though a resident of Biddeford Pool, had grown up in Saco and graduated from Thornton Academy. However, these two strikes against the mayoral candidate did not stop him from running. He won with 41 percent of the vote. He had proved the naysayers wrong, and some believe "Nutting's mayoral win was the result of a 'perfect political storm,' in which several key issues converged into a mass of voter resentment about politics."[185]

Biddeford had grown tired of stagnant leadership. Nutting wanted to take an active approach. This concept was proven within weeks of his election. Nutting's schedule was busy "brushing up on a multitude of ongoing issues and extensive tours of every city department" as well as the businesses downtown.[186] On the first of many walking tours, Nutting and the current economic development director, Robert Dodge, visited Langevin's, Oak Point Associates, Warren's Furniture, Pot de Fleur, Maternity Fair and Youland's Jewelers. (Oak Point is the only business still in existence.) When Nutting met Newell Potter, owner of Warren's, he learned of the businessman's doubt that Biddeford would ever bustle again. Potter criticized the city for "wanting to have both eggs. They

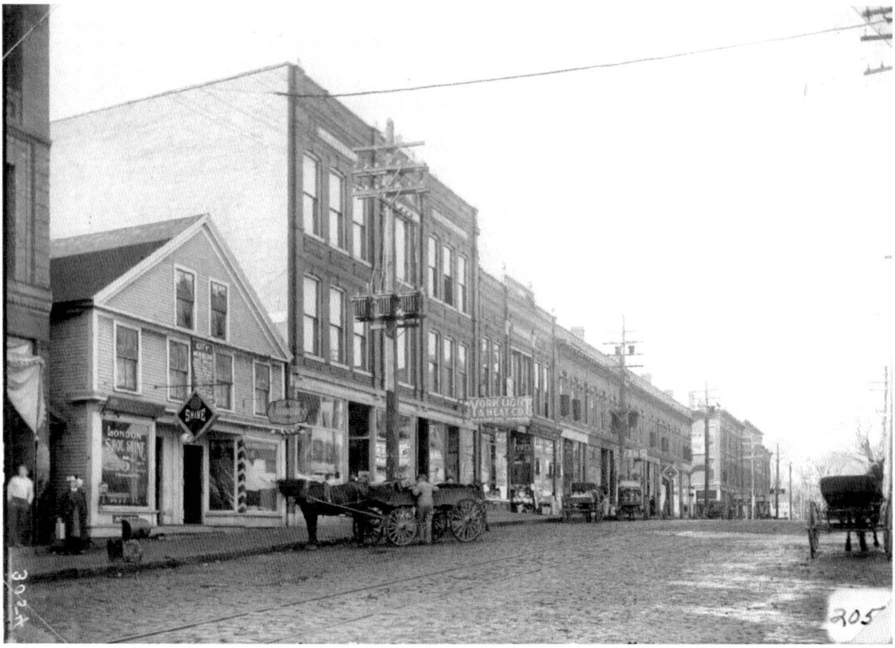

A view of Main Street and its many businesses looking toward Elm Street, circa 1909. *McArthur Public Library Archive.*

want places like Wal-Mart and all the taxes and the downtown too."[187] Unfortunately, consumers had shifted shopping habits away from small businesses, finding better bargains at box stores. This left the few remaining shops on Main Street often empty, and even places like Reny's wanted to move out of downtown to a new location with better exposure and more parking.

By listening to residents and business owners, Nutting "became an ambassador of goodwill and a cheerleader for promoting Biddeford's potential" during his tenure as mayor.[188] Through these conversations, the mayor spearheaded a task force to focus on the revitalization of downtown Biddeford. This group was not intended to be a committee or commission of the city, but rather a separate organization with a mission to both promote existing businesses and attract new business downtown. Early volunteers in the group included David Flood, founder and editor of the *Biddeford-Saco-OOB Courier*; Renee O'Neill, director of City Theater; and Donna Tippett, the city's planning director. Tippett would serve as interim director for the group, newly dubbed "Heart of Biddeford." Nutting introduced these individuals to the Downtown Development Commission during a June 30,

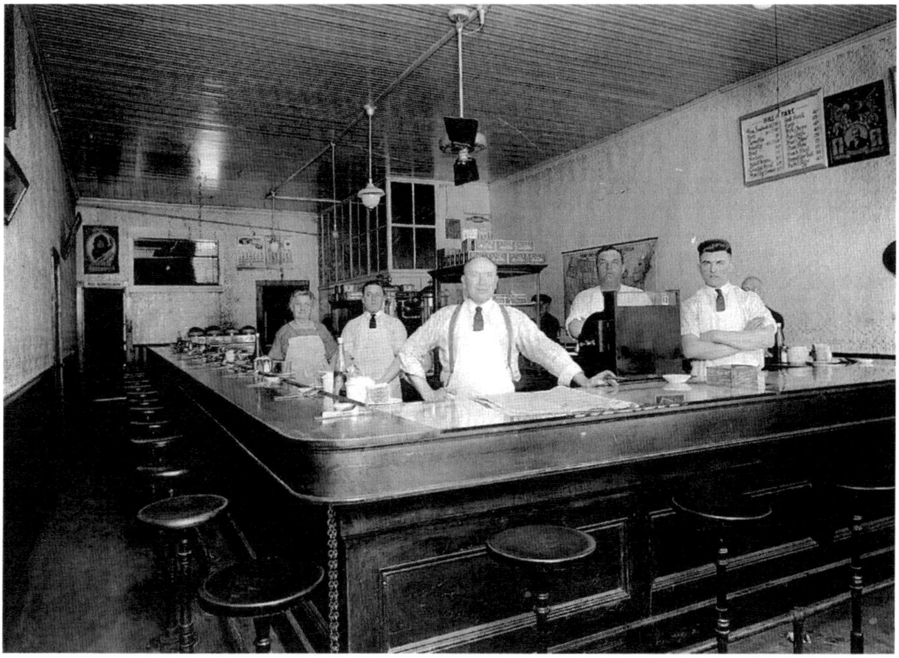

At the Imperial Café on Alfred Street, you could order fried claims for twenty-five cents or a large steak for sixty-five cents. Pictured in the café is owner Leon Baiguy with his employees, circa 1916. *McArthur Public Library Archive.*

2004 meeting. At this juncture, the group sought to solicit city funding of $20,000 annually with contributions from downtown businesses and private donors, with the mission to become designated as a nonprofit and Main Street Maine community.[189] The Heart of Biddeford aimed to follow guidelines set forth by the National Main Street Center, a program founded in 1980 by the National Trust for Historic Preservation aimed at helping historic communities across the country renew and revitalize downtown districts.

During the meeting, Bonita Pothier explained how Saco developed a similar program, which had been running for approximately three years. At the time, Saco had approximately 120 businesses that "all work together to create a winning attitude."[190] Though there was hesitation at first, the fact that developers had started to purchase vacant mill buildings and the city's downtown economy continued to struggle prompted many to agree that something must be done. It took the initial members a year to receive the Main Street Maine designation, at which time they hired Rachael Weyand as a part-time director to run the organization, opening a small office in a city-owned storefront on Main Street.

As Heart of Biddeford developed its mission, a developer took interest in the abandoned brick buildings lining the Saco River. Doug Sanford, who had purchased the old Woolworth's block in 1982, was investing in real estate again through the purchase of North Dam Mill in 2004. The property consisted of three five-story buildings, interconnected and spanning 370,000 square feet.[191] Like key figures in Biddeford's history, Sanford saw potential in the city's downtown and the historic, structurally sound mills, as well as in the picturesque riverfront and beach access. Having Southern Maine Health Center and the University of New England in the community was an added bonus.[192] According to Sanford, "There are a number of assets that a vibrant community has to have and they are all [in Biddeford]."[193] Many did not understand Sanford's motive: "No one wanted to be in Biddeford…people would ask me if I was crazy."[194] And maybe he was, because Biddeford faced many hurdles in the next few years, fighting to overcome a negative perception and impacted, yet again, by a national recession.

21

THE LAST BLANKET

As with most communities across the country, the national recession in 2008 impacted Biddeford's remaining industry. After many years of outsourcing and a slow loss of jobs, 2009 marked the end of Biddeford textile operations. WestPoint Home notified the 121 remaining employees that it would shutter its operations in the city.[195] The closure of the last textile operation seemed inevitable to the city manager, John Bubier. He told Mainebiz, "This is simply something we had anticipated. It was a question of when, not whether."[196] However, as WestPoint employees clocked out of their shift for the last time, a renaissance was already brewing. Bubier said, "No one wants to see a neighbor out of a job, but Biddeford has to work hard to shed the stigma of a stagnant mill town."[197]

When the news hit of WestPoint Home's closure, the city had already begun assessing the downtown mills to develop a master plan for redevelopment. During the creation of the assessment, the city looked at options with WestPoint Home machines still spinning and, alternatively, with the textile manufacturing company closed for good. The goal, according to an October 2009 report, was to "strategically guide new private and public investment in the site with recommendations for" a mixture of residential, retail and commercial businesses using the abundant space.[198] There was also emphasis placed on infrastructure of the city, improved access to the river views and attention to the heritage of the mills. The thirty-eight-acre span of mill buildings and mill property flanking the Saco River is listed in the National Register of Historic Places. While that classification opens up

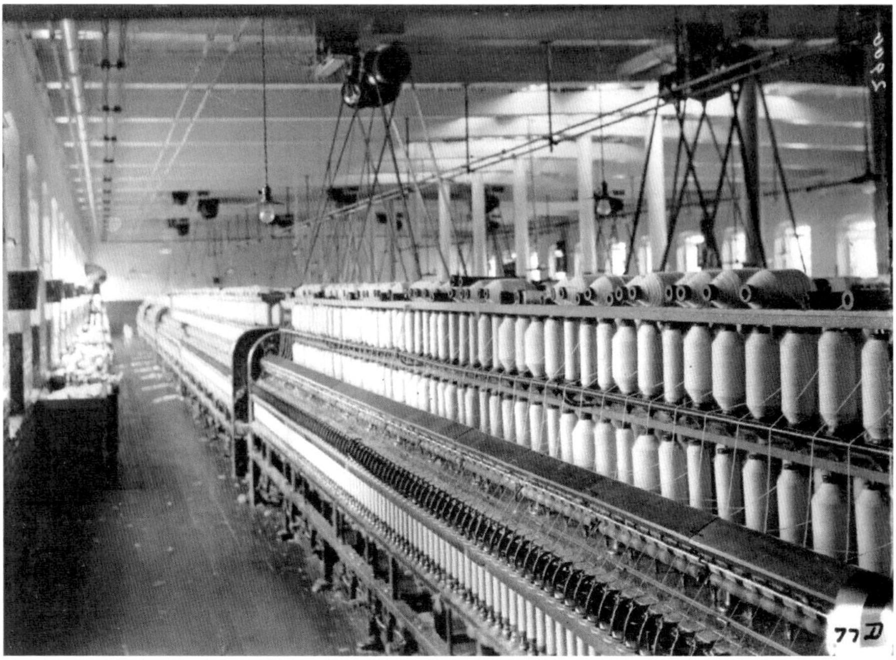

A spinning room at Pepperell Manufacturing Company's Laconia Division in December 1910. *Robert H. Gay Photograph Collection, courtesy of McArthur Public Library.*

special funding and tax credits, city officials on both sides of the river did not want to move forward with reimagining the empty mills without considering the rich history within those walls.

By the time the report was released to the public, WestPoint Home had vacated a building with approximately 675,000 square feet of usable space. Sanford, who had already renovated a portion of North Dam Mill for business and residential use, would ultimately acquire the WestPoint Home property, as well. Additionally, early plans were in place to convert Riverdam Mill into workforce housing and, light industrial and manufacturing businesses found space to work in Lincoln and Bugbee Brown mill buildings. The slow redevelopment of the mills created a buzz about town and attracted newcomers to the area. Entrepreneurs like graphic designer Tammy Ackerman, artists Coco and Gil Corral and architect Caleb Johnson, as well as additional developers, including Chris Betjemann, found themselves attracted to Biddeford's vibe. When Johnson's wife enrolled at the University of New England, the couple relocated to the area. Johnson recalled, "We drove into downtown and I loved it…then we drove out to Biddeford Pool and there were surfers sitting out on the swells. That clinched it for me," even though the city's low-income neighborhoods fueled the lack of economic and cultural diversity.[199]

The one thing that remained wholly unchanged through the course of Biddeford's history was the quality of its people. Early leaders who wanted to attract business to the city pointed to the hardworking residents, and Betjemann believes "they're people who could hold their own anywhere" with "tremendous talent and a positive energy.[200] That very sentiment spurred Heart of Biddeford members to seek community input in identifying goals for revitalizing the downtown district. The nonprofit group recognized that "a mix of newcomers and longer-term residents [had] begun to realize the potential of Biddeford as an economic and cultural center again," and they hoped to capture that through a storytelling project called "HeartSpots: Downtown's Memory Lane."[201]

A collaborative effort between city officials and Heart of Biddeford, the project kicked off during the 2009 La Kermesse festival. Organizers sought to engage as many of Biddeford's twenty-one-thousand-plus residents as possible. To do so, the city officials and volunteers would conduct interviews, host neighborhood meetings and plan community forums and workshops. With the assistance of Salt Institute for Documentary Studies fellows, over one hundred interviews were conducted and the voices of community members heard. From that point, thirty-five neighborhood meetings were organized, garnering input from over three hundred residents. The conversations boiled down to key values important to these community members, which included historic preservation, fostering a family-friendly and diverse city, and supporting a creative economy to help revitalize the empty Main Street and mills, all without losing the charm of a small-town atmosphere.[202]

Additionally, community members helped city officials take a hard look at concerns. Residents were worried about public safety. A need to improve the city's infrastructure and create a more welcoming appearance downtown was critical in welcoming visitors from neighboring towns and tourists who flood coastal Maine during the summer. Residents also expressed the value of the city's youth, offering them a place and voice in the community, as well.

After three years of community networking, a report by the Orton Family Foundation notes:

> *Biddeford accepted a new Downtown Master Plan that puts its community values front and center and ties priority actions to them. For some, change will still be hard. Even with more success downtown, some people continue*

> *to question how the city can recover or whether that recovery will come at the expense of those who came before.* [203]

Luckily for Biddeford, the innovators and dreamers finally began to outweigh the naysayers, and the agents of change were already in motion.

22

Goodbye "Trash Town"

When Biddeford welcomed Maine Energy Recovery Company to its downtown in 1987, officials hoped it would help the city's suffering economy. However, the trash incinerator had meant nothing but problems from the start. Regular complaints of an overpowering odor were received at city hall from residents of both Biddeford and neighboring Saco. Longtime residents were fed up with the stigma it developed in town, and newcomers were likewise concerned with its presence. Tammy Ackerman, who had developed the arts nonprofit organization Engine since arriving in the city, could not "advocate having a trash incinerator in a town with so much potential. It doesn't fit the direction the town wants to go."[204] To many, it was also the biggest obstacle blocking the road to revitalization.

During a June 2011 public meeting with the Department of Environmental Protection, a proposed license renewal for Maine Energy Recovery Company was considered. Thirty residents were present; all of them voiced strong opinions against the downtown trash incinerator.[205] Downtown property owner and Main Street resident Chris Betjemann admitted the stench had improved, "but it still stinks probably once a week. [The current regulation] is not working. Please, we need some help."[206] The residents' concerns had not changed over the course of Maine Energy Recovery's history in Biddeford, and within another year, a proposed buyout went before city councilors. Finally, after twenty-five years of trash being hauled through downtown, officials approved a $6.65 million deal with Casella Waste Systems to purchase the incinerator and close it for good.

The closure would result in the loss of seventy-five downtown jobs, but it would ultimately create more potential by opening up nearly nine acres of riverfront property.[207]

Mayor Alan Casavant called Maine Energy Recovery Company "a big blue obstacle to redevelopment of the city's former textile mills into residential, retail and manufacturing spaces."[208] Guy Gagnon, the director of the Biddeford Housing Authority, echoed the mayor's sentiment. He said,

> *For 30 years, Biddeford-Saco has served communities from all over the region by allowing trash to be trucked to the center of town. While we have welcomed taking on the responsibility of solving trash issues for the region, the result has been to depress the region and prevent real economic growth from occurring in an area that is ripe for growth.*[209]

Both men agreed that Biddeford could no longer be dubbed "Trash Town, U.S.A."[210]

Once the last trash was processed at Maine Energy Recover Company and the incinerator shut down for good, city crews worked to clean up the

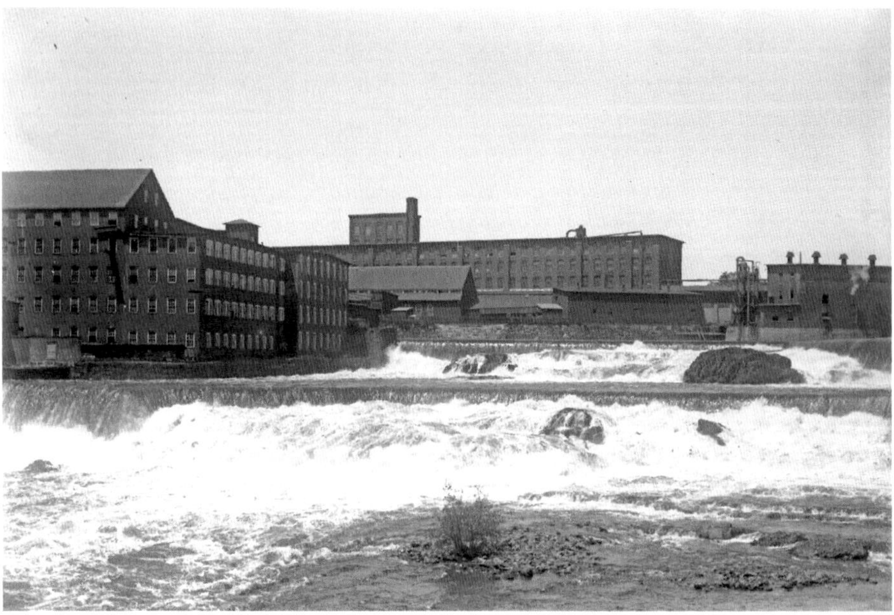

The Pepperell and York mills can be seen along the Saco River falls from the Main Street bridge, prior to the power plant's construction on the Biddeford side of the river, circa 1912. *McArthur Public Library Archive.*

site, and officials began brainstorming ideas for the large parcel of land in the heart of the city. Nathan Szanton, the developer who renovated a mill building and opened the Lofts at Saco Falls in the fall of 2016, said, "[Maine Energy] was a wet blanket on development in downtown Biddeford. The constant presence of trash trucks, the odor of the trucks and the emissions from the stack were a ball and chain around the legs of Biddeford. To have that chain snapped allows Biddeford to run."[211] And run it did; within three years, vacancy on Main Street dropped 37 percent, and more than $70 million in new projects, including Szanton's lofts, was approved in the mill district.[212]

Since the purchase of the Maine Energy Recovery Company property, the city has examined potential avenues for redevelopment of the site. Camoin Associates, a New York–based firm, suggested creating a mix of commercial, retail and residential space for the area while keeping the city's needs in mind.[213] All that remains of the incinerator today is the domineering smokestack, which the city opted to keep as a means of generating income through the existing cell towers positioned on the structure.[214] Aside from the smokestack, the property is largely a blank slate for reinventing a prime portion of the city's downtown situated along the falls of the Saco River.

23

Biddeford Begins Bustling

According to the city's economic and community development director Daniel Stevenson, "The buyout of the Maine Energy site was a transformative event for the downtown."[215] While most agree with Stevenson, additional factors were at play, including an influx of new residents attracted by the city's vibe; affordable living and commercial space; improving local and national economies; as well as the opening of unique coffee shops, boutiques and other businesses in the downtown.[216]

The addition of businesses filling up Biddeford's storefronts is thanks in part to initiatives put in place through Heart of Biddeford. Just prior to the buyout of Maine Energy Recovery Company, the nonprofit organized a contest to fill available commercial space and join the likes of longtime businesses such as Reilly's Bakery, New Morning Natural Foods and La Corseterie, to name a few. With the Main Street Challenge, the organization solicited business pitches from near and far hoping to attract an array of ideas for viable storefronts. The first call for pitches in 2012 received twenty-seven proposals. The second challenge held the following year garnered seventeen proposals. In each round, ten entrepreneurs were asked to submit formal business plans for review. A fraction of these plans were selected for a more formal interview process. Three finalists each year were chosen to open a business downtown. Winners of both challenges received a large prize package, including a $10,000 forgivable loan and a $10,000 value of business-related services such as logo design, web development, accounting and legal advice. Additionally, these businesses were given a wide range of spaces from which to choose in order to open up shop.[217]

In 2012, the three businesses to open were a retail space for Tote Road, an already existing hand-carved woodworking business; Dahlia's Delights, a new vegetarian café; and Elements: Books Coffee Beer, a trifecta that has turned into one of Biddeford's hottest hangouts.[218] The three business plans chosen in the 2013 Main Street Challenge included the opening of a storefront for Desert Moon Leather, a handmade leather goods business; Biscuits & Company, a new bakery concept devoted to biscuits and other yummy goods; and a microbrewery.[219] Of the six businesses, three remain open and successful: Desert Moon, Elements and Biscuits & Company. While the microbrewery ultimately never came to fruition, forfeiting the prize, and the other two businesses have since closed, the Main Street Challenge proved successful in drawing interest to Biddeford's downtown. Other national Main Street organizations have utilized the plan as a business incubator for their cities. Meanwhile, Biscuits & Company and Elements continue to be featured in statewide and national press, drawing customers from neighboring towns and even Portland, as well as welcoming summer tourists into the downtown area previously passed by on their arrivals into town.

The new businesses have resurrected the vibrant energy that once was Biddeford's bustling downtown. According to Caleb Johnson, "the image has changed." Johnson's architectural firm is now run out of a renovated Main Street building where Elements is located, with other properties on tap for reimagining, including the old courthouse and a shuttered Bank of America branch.[220] "The people who are working here are proud of it and like being on the fringe and outside of the established touristy spots like Portland and Kennebunkport," said Johnson. He anticipates the city's full transformation will be complete within another ten or fifteen years. Since the closure of Maine Energy Recover Company, "more than $65 million in new projects has been completed or is underway," and that is exactly the type of economic shift Biddeford needs.[221]

24

The Pepperell Mill Campus

The most recent housing project to open in Biddeford is an eighty-unit housing complex, The Lofts at Saco Falls, which opened in September 2016. Szanton announced this mill renovation project shortly after the Maine Energy Recovery Company was bought out. Before the project was complete, seventy of the units were rented; the remaining ten vacancies were filled within a week.

While the Lofts are the latest renovation project, much credit goes to Doug Sanford when talking about the brick "pyramids" of Biddeford. Since his 2004 purchase of North Dam Mill, Sanford has continued buying buildings and renovating sections at a time. With his latest acquisition of the WestPoint Homes property, his company, Pepperell Mill Campus, now manages 1.1 million square feet of mill space.[222] When he first invested in Biddeford, Sanford said, "People would ask me if I was crazy. Did I ever imagine this? No....We had some obstacles. [The trash incinerator] was a big one. It made it a really tough sell to any real job creation or folks who would invest in this community."[223]

According to an October 2016 newsletter, the Pepperell Mill Campus has allowed for 120 businesses to move into the once-abandoned mills.[224] Some of these businesses honor the textile heritage of Biddeford's past, including Angelrox, a women's clothing brand sold in over two hundred boutiques nationwide, and Hyperlite Mountain Gear, which fashions a wide array of outdoor gear from lightweight, high-tech fabrics. In addition to these businesses, the campus is home to Banded Horn Brewery, Round Turn

Distillery, an indoor playground for children called The Yard, a franchise location of Maine's Portland Pie, a homemade ice cream stand called Sweet Cream Dairy, Tulu Hair Salon and Maine Juice Company. And the list goes on and on. Since 2012 alone, Sanford has invested $5.6 million in the city, with no plans to stop any time soon.[225]

Sanford's early vision of creating a hub for people to live, work and enjoy life has finally come to fruition, with room to flourish. People once thought he was crazy for investing in such a downtrodden community, but Sanford can now confidently say that "the development that's been taking place downtown and in the mills has moved beyond mere speculation."[226] With approximately 40 percent of Pepperell Mill Campus already renovated and in use for a variety of purposes, Sanford and his crew are updating the campus's master plan to reflect the potential purposes of the remaining property.

25

Challenges of Growth

With marked progress, the visionaries have been able to move past the people who claimed Biddeford's comeback was impossible. However, as the founders of Pepperell Manufacturing Company faced various challenges, so have the developers and city officials who encountered the trials that come with urban growth and revitalization.

After a decade of hard work, it seems Biddeford has overcome the run-down perception that was pervasive during the 1990s and early twenty-first century. Former city manager John Bubier believes that "Biddeford has gone from a negative image to a place where people are willing to poke their nose into the community to see what's here."[227] Unfortunately, there is still not sufficient action downtown to keep establishments busy enough to be profitable. When Chad Conley and Greg Mitchell took over the nearly century-old Palace Diner, the duo took a stab at serving a limited dinner menu in addition to the breakfast and lunch shift that regulars at the diner were accustomed to. While their plates got rave reviews, the city can become "a ghost town" at night. According to Mitchell, "it's like a two-steps-forward, one-step-back scenario" and he admitted the city is at an "interesting juncture…with any city that's developing, there are pros and cons."[228]

One major con that the city has continually faced is easily accessible, readily available parking. In fact, during the 1954 annual report, Mayor Louis B. Lausier noted that "parking in the business district becomes a greater problem as the years go by. As the city spreads out, more and more shoppers are forced to depend on the use of their cars for shopping."[229] Sixty

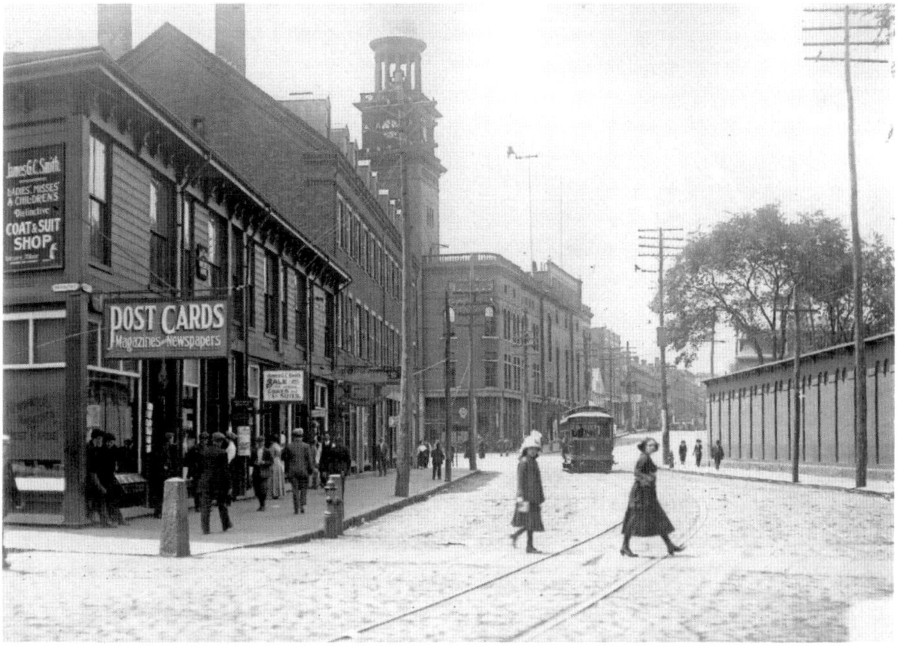

A trolley runs down Main Street near the intersection of Washington Street as ladies cross toward the mills, circa 1912. *McArthur Public Library Archive.*

years later, the issue is pervasive. People used to walk from their apartments to the mills for work. Now, people who live in the mills need cars to commute to their jobs; conversely, people who work downtown need reliable parking during business hours that will not interfere with customer parking.

The lack of parking has stymied some of Biddeford's regrowth. In 2016, two companies that could have added seven hundred jobs downtown opted to locate operations elsewhere, citing parking as a major reason for not choosing Biddeford. Since assuming his elected position as mayor, Alan Casavant has pushed the matter to the forefront. When the concept of a parking garage for downtown residents and employees was broached in 2012, the idea was met with extreme opposition. Some against the idea did not feel the city should foot the bill for mill parking. Others did not want the burden to fall to taxpayers who have seen ever-increasing property taxes over the course of the city's recent history. The strong opposition even prompted a citywide referendum in which voters successfully banned the potential for parking meters along Main Street and other major downtown roads. For Casavant, addressing parking is no longer a matter of if, but how. He indicated that the city is "at a crossroads. To maximize

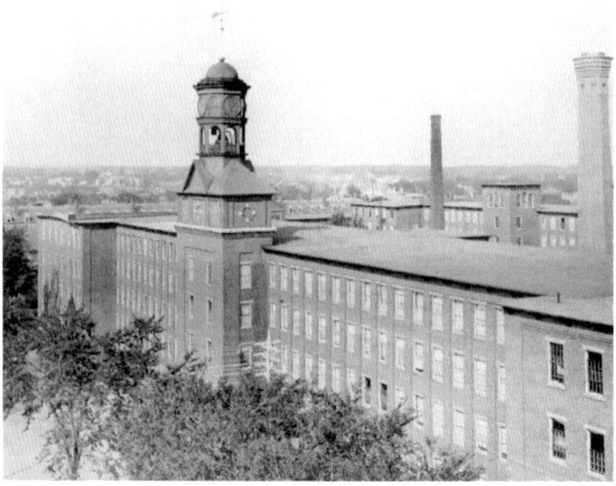

Pepperell Manufacturing Company's Lincoln Street mill as seen from city hall. *McArthur Public Library Archive.*

development and stabilize taxes, we have to have the parking infrastructure downtown."[230]

Meanwhile, city officials also hope to improve the "walkability" of downtown. City councilors approved a sidewalk reconstruction project in September 2016. Crews quickly got to work tearing up sidewalks along lower Main Street. The project's goal was to address overgrown tree roots that were undermining the structural integrity of the sidewalks, as well as replacing sewer lines and streetlights.[231] While it is hard to disagree with projects that better the overall appearance of the city, business owners struggled to meet sales goals during the course of the project. Crews blocked off the majority of on-street parking, and the torn-up walkways made access to storefronts difficult. However, City Manager Jim Bennett argues that the short-term inconveniences will prove worth it in the long run, because "[new] sidewalks and other things…are going to impact the kinds of people that will be in the downtown."[232]

On the whole, the investors purchasing property downtown have largely utilized vacant buildings for housing and commercial projects. However, a 2015 planning board approval allowing developer Tim Harrington to overhaul the old Lincoln Mill displaced fifteen businesses with very little notice. Sergey Fisenko Inc., a builder of custom kitchens, had worked out of the mill for thirteen years. Owner Sergey Fisenko admitted, "The redevelopment is nice for everybody else…[but] I'm scared to death. I don't have a place to go."[233] Another business owner, Michael Ventura, "has no hard feelings," as he figured, "the end was coming soon anyway…the building is pretty rundown."[234] Aside from the gradual closure of textile mills, this ousting is likely one of the largest to occur during the course of mill renovations to date. However difficult, city officials and the developer hold out hope that the decision to evict businesses from the old mill will prove beneficial to the downtown as a whole.[235]

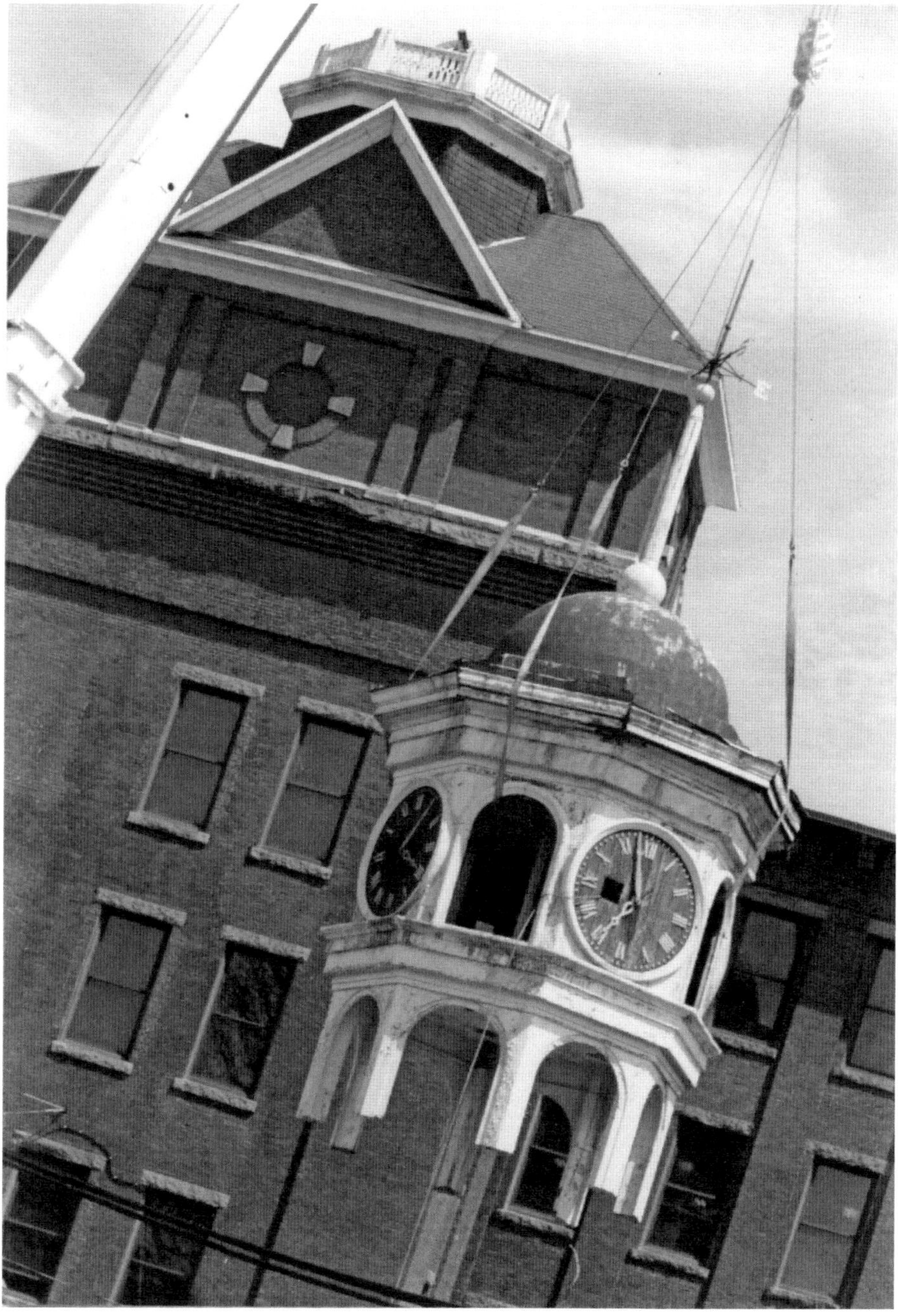

A clock tower atop Pepperell Manufacturing Company's Mill No. 3 on Lincoln Street was removed in 2007 due to deteriorating conditions. *Raymond Gaudette photo, courtesy of McArthur Library.*

26

Four Hundred Years Later

When Vines and his thirty-two men arrived in Saco Bay, they focused on surviving the winter. During the 2016 Independence Day festivities in Biddeford Pool, community members marked the quadricentennial of Vines's arrival and founding of Winter Harbor. A group of men portrayed the English crew rowing ashore to the welcome of Sokoki tribesmen. In the fall, the Biddeford Historical Society marked the anniversary with a full day of presentations at the First Parish Meetinghouse, the original meetinghouse for the town. Presenters included Mayor Casavant and historical society members Paul McDonough and Charles Butler.[236] More than two centuries after early settlers first arrived, Batchelder saw unmatched potential in the property on the western bank of the Saco River. Today, another generation of visionaries works together as Biddeford forges on into its fifth century, reimagined, reborn and revitalizing.

While a monument at Leighton's Point commemorates Vines's settlement, a banner hangs along the side of the defunct mill building at the corner of Lincoln and Main Streets advertising the $65 million project, "The New Lincoln Mill." After years of plight, the city is seeing commercial buildings sell "on average, nearly 59 percent above assessed value…residential properties are selling for 12 percent above assessed value."[237] In addition to the successful real estate sales figures, the 2010 U.S. census revealed the city's median age is thirty-four years old, nearly ten years younger than the statewide median age of forty-three and a half, proving Biddeford has successfully attracted a young, energetic demographic.[238] Bennett attributes

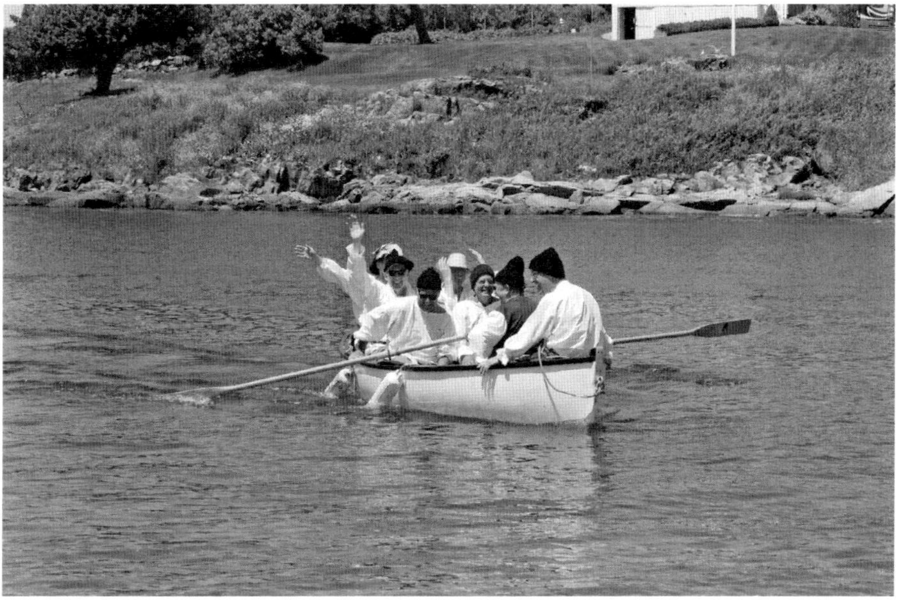

Reenactors row ashore during the July 4, 2016 quadricentennial celebration of Captain Richard Vines's arrival and founding of Winter Harbor, now known as Biddeford Pool. *Janice Hamilton photo.*

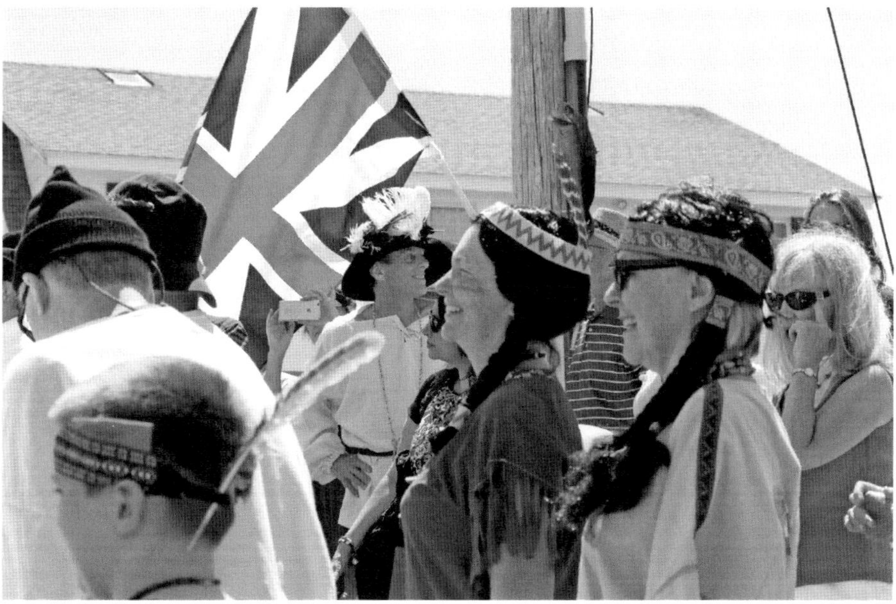

Reenactors dressed as English explorers and members of the Sokoki tribe help celebrate the four hundredth anniversary of Captain Richard Vines's arrival. *Janice Hamilton photo.*

this to the "buzz" Biddeford is generating. He said, "The community has a raw 'it' factor that's attracting people to the city."[239]

Machines are still thrumming in the mill, but now these are the sounds of juice presses, high-end industrial sewing machines, brewery equipment and more. While the practical needs for cloth drove the early textile industry in Biddeford, the turn to a creative economy has helped resurrect a downtown struggling to survive. This change has been slow and not always universally embraced. However, it is hard to ignore the new additions, regular press coverage and ever-increasing interest in Biddeford. Many who remember Biddeford's former heyday are watching the progress unfold with mixed emotions. Lifelong resident and former director of the historical society Norman Beaupré finds the redevelopment rather exciting. He sees the changes over the past decade as incredibly positive: "It has always been a great difficulty for Biddeford to get away from [the stereotype of] a Franco American mill city."[240] However, he appreciates the value placed on the city's history while progress is pursued. After all, he said, "I do not think you can grow economically or culturally if we do not appreciate the past."[241]

EPILOGUE

DELILAH POUPORE

In 2007, my husband and I moved back to his home state, Maine. He grew up in Sanford and Shapleigh. We stayed with his family at first. We visited many towns and cities along the coast, seeking a walkable, affordable community to call our home.

The expansive brick textile mill buildings on either side of the Saco River falls drew our interest to Biddeford and Saco. Ultimately, we purchased a home on the east side of the river, but the goings-on to the west side of the river kept us returning to Biddeford. We explored the downtown during Friday night art walks, attended events at McArthur Library and shopped at

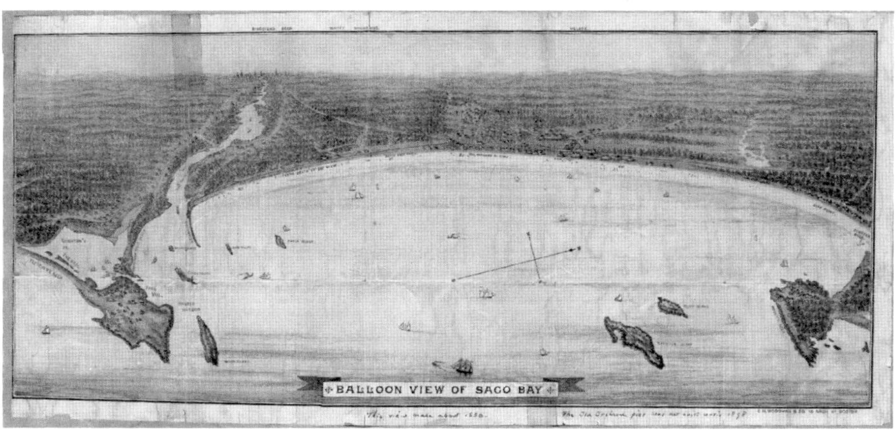

A hand-drawn view of the river and Saco Bay prior to the construction of the famed Pier in Old Orchard Beach, circa 1880. *McArthur Public Library Archive.*

a children's clothing store on Main Street. The small ethnic restaurants on Main and Alfred Streets became quick favorites. I played gigs in quaint coffee shops. Having grown up in Minnesota and lived in various cities across the country, we appreciated that Biddeford was easily approachable and offered many amenities that could be found in a larger city.

Then, Heart of Biddeford launched its "Heart and Soul" community listening project. I was so intrigued by the concept of a community seeking input from its members to make plans for the city's future. The program welcomed residents of all ages—from those who had lived in Biddeford for their entire life to newcomers—to talk about what they loved about Biddeford, why they are drawn to the city and even why they never left. The project inspired me to apply when Heart of Biddeford sought an interim director in 2011 to lead the organization.

In my years working for Heart of Biddeford, I learned more about residents' passion for this city and its deeply rooted history. Combined, this has led to the renovation of City Theater, the formation of a Main Street program, cultivation of a creative economy, rehabilitation of century-old buildings and the foundation of a mills museum. Over the past decade, I have watched Biddeford be reborn.

The revitalization of this community has, in part, been successful thanks to an innovative spirit. However, I admire the respect for the city's history and the desire to preserve the foundation on which the city was built. Developers chose to avoid urban renewal through extensive renovations of solidly built mill buildings that have withstood the test of time. These buildings where the majority of Biddeford's residents worked are now home to many newcomers and a variety of entrepreneurial businesses. The buildings form a bustling hub for commerce and community. In essence, the same innovation Samuel Batchelder introduced when he founded the Pepperell Manufacturing Company has led Biddeford to experience a boom of new business, the creation of numerous jobs formerly lost when the mills closed, a whole new housing market and expanded cultural offerings—all of which are creating a vibrant downtown Biddeford once again. Textile products from high-end women's clothing to hardy camping gear are still being produced within the mills' walls. Additionally, craft businesses, including breweries, a distillery, a coffee/beer/bookshop, an organic juice company, a leather craftsman, a women's lingerie shop and a fourth-generation-run bakery bring Biddeford full circle to a time nearly two hundred years ago when small businesses popped up and prospered. The difference today is that Biddeford draws attention statewide and nationally. Eateries have been featured in magazines like *Bon Appétit*. Women take the train from Boston and New York to shop in quaint boutiques and visit the beautiful beaches. Performances at City Theater draw crowds reminiscent of the days of Eva Gray. The millennial generation is drawn to the vibe created by Biddeford's growing economy.

As Biddeford forges forward, I hope the city can also continue to honor its working-class history while creating opportunities in the new economy. While we have successfully avoided urban renewal, those of us struggling to build connection across economic divides also want to avoid gentrification of a community built by hard workers. While the city has grown its appeal to people who own summer homes in Biddeford Pool and those who can afford a week's vacation in a beach house, we also need to remember the families living in former tenement homes and create opportunity for them, as well.

Biddeford has evolved in the past decade, and there is no shortage of opinions on what this city ought to be. Thankfully, there is no shortage of people willing to make a difference, from the hundreds of volunteers who support organizations such as Heart of Biddeford, Engine, City Theater, Biddeford Mills Museum, McArthur Library, Seeds of Hope and the food pantries, to the city personnel and elected officials who invest their time and ideas into the city's inner workings. The people of Biddeford are creating an exciting future for this city—one park cleanup, one parade, one festival, one grand opening, many a conversation and great idea at a time. We continue to weave new threads into our already fascinating history.

Delilah Poupore is the executive director of Heart of Biddeford, a Main Street Maine organization dedicated to the revitalization of the city's downtown.

Appendix

The Mayors of Biddeford

In 1855, the City of Biddeford enacted its first charter and elected its first mayor. While the mayoral election is not run by political parties, throughout the town's history, candidates have identified as Democrat (D),

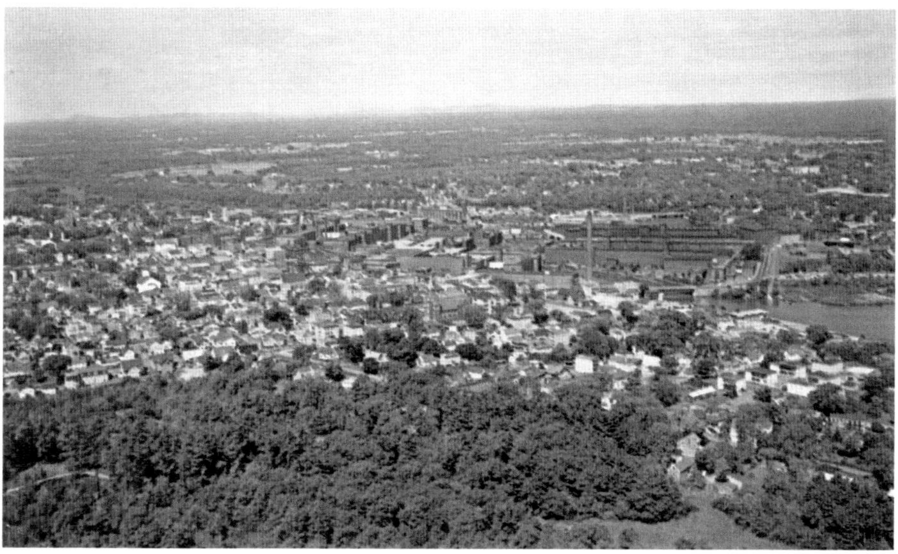

An aerial view of Biddeford's downtown, circa 1973. *Don Sieburg photo, courtesy of McArthur Library.*

Republican (R), Citizen (C), Independent (I) or Progressive (P). The city's sixtieth mayor, Alan Casavant, was elected for his third two-year term in November 2015.

Daniel E. Somes (R) 1855–56
James Andrews (R) 1857
Cyrus Gordon (D) 1858–59
Jonathan Tuck (D) 1860
Esreff H. Banks (R) 1860
Seth S. Fairfield (D) 1861–62
John Q. Adams (D) 1863–64
Charles A. Shaw (D) 1865–66
Ferguson Haines (D) 1867–68
James R. Clark (D) 1869
E.W. Wedgewood (D) 1870–71
Francis G. Warren (D) 1872
James H. McMullan (R) 1873
Francis G. Warren (D) 1874–75
John H. Burnham (D) 1876
Alfred Pierce (R) 1877
Charles M. Moses (R) 1878
James A. Strout (D) 1879
Charles M. Moses (R) 1880
Elisha E. Clark (R) 1881–82
E.W. Staples (D) 1883–85
Samuel F. Parcher (D) 1886–87
C.E. Goodwin (D) 1888–89
E.W. Staples (D) 1890–93
Charles S. Hamilton (R) 1894–95
Carlos Heard (C & D) 1896–97
Levi W. Stone (C & R) 1898–99
Nathaniel B. Walker (C, R & D) 1900–1
Joseph Gooch (C, R & D) 1902–3
Nathaniel B. Walker (C & R) 1904–5
Gilman P. Littlefield (C & R) 1906–7
Cornelius Horigan (D & I) 1908–9
Albert O. Marcille (D & I) 1910–12
James G.C. Smith (D & I) 1913–15
Leopold A. Girard (D & I) 1916
Hartley C. Banks (D & I) 1917–19
Thomas F. Locke (D & I) 1920
Ulysses B. Fosdick (R & C) 1921
Edward H. Drapeau (D & I) 1922–25
George C. Precourt (R & P) 1926–29
Cornelius Horigan (D & I) 1930–31
Jerome A. Morin (R & P) 1932–33
George E. Beauchesne (P) 1934
Arthur J. Remillard (D) 1935–36
Frederick H. Mitchell (D) 1936–37
Wilfrid Landry (D) 1937–40
Louis B. Lausier (D) 1941–54
Albert Lambert (D) 1955–57
Clement Deschambeault (D) 1958–62
Willie Pomerleau (R) 1963–64
Edward Gaulin (D) 1965
Leo R. Lemire (D) 1966–69
Gilbert R. Boucher (D) 1970–73
Lucien A. Dutremble (D) 1974–79
Roger L. Frechette (D) 1980–81
Martin J. Reilly (D) 1982–83
Robert M. Farley (D) 1984–85
Martin J. Reilly (D) 1986–87
Michael P. Cantara (D) 1988–89
Bonita P. Belanger (D) 1990–91
Roger Normand (D) 1992–93
James Grattelo (D) 1994–97
Donna Dion (D) 1998–2003
Wallace Nutting (R) 2004–7
JoAnne Twomey (D) 2008–11
Alan Casavant (D) 2012–present

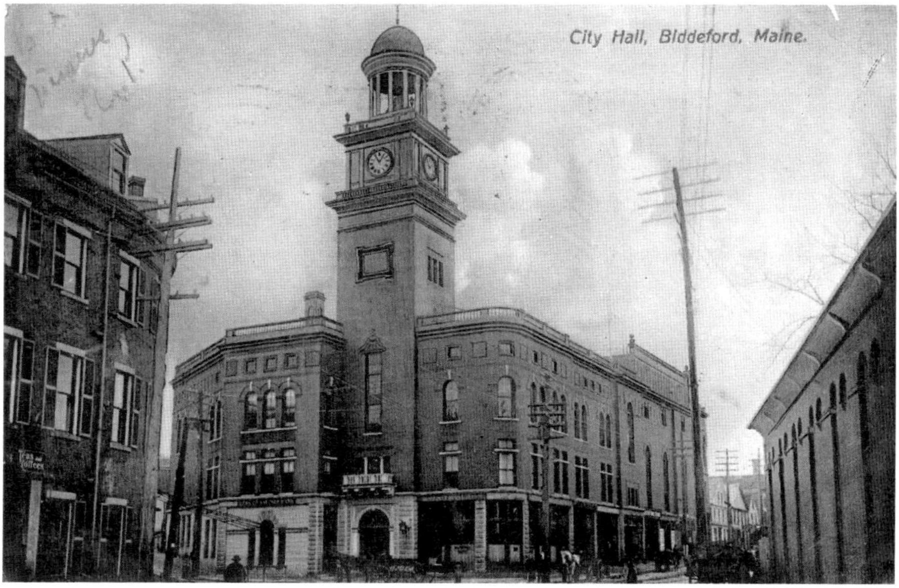

A view of Biddeford City Hall. *McArthur Public Library Archive.*

THE MILLS OF BIDDEFORD

Biddeford's expansive mill district has served as a blank canvas for business owners and investors. At the time of a 2009 survey, some thirty-five buildings were counted as part of the mill district, most of which were built prior to 1900 utilizing massive wood beams from Maine's forests, bricks produced along the Saco River and granite hauled from Biddeford quarries. These solid structures serve as the backbone on which Biddeford's future is being reimagined and rebuilt. Below is a current list of buildings and status of use.

Pepperell Mill Campus consists of WestPoint Stevens's 8.9-acre property and North Dam's 4.4-acre property. The campus encompasses fifteen buildings, totaling just shy of one million square feet, and in the following states:

Building 9, fully occupied
Building 11, vacant
Building 12, vacant
Building 13, fully renovated and half occupied, including commercial, office and light manufacturing
Building 13W, fully occupied with light manufacturing

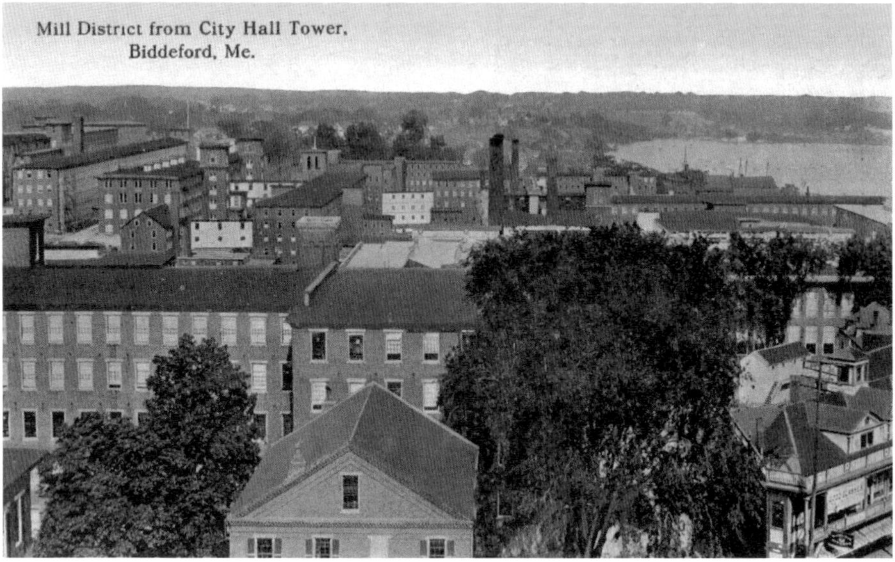

An aerial view of the mill district from the city hall clock tower, circa 1910. *Richard N. Carr Collection, courtesy of McArthur Public Library.*

Building 15, one-third occupied with light manufacturing
Building 16, demolished for additional parking
Building 17, renovated and fully occupied with commercial and office space
Building 18, renovated and fully occupied with commercial and office space
Building 19, vacant
Building 20, vacant
Building 30, fully occupied
Building 35, renovated and fully occupied, residential
Building 36, storage facility
Building 37, fully occupied

In addition to the Pepperell Mill Campus, the following buildings within the mill district are in use for residential, business or manufacturing purposes:

Mill at Saco Falls, 60,000 square feet, renovated and fully occupied residential
Lofts at Saco Falls, 65,000 square feet, renovated and fully occupied residential
River Dam, 90,000 square feet, partially occupied
Bugbee Brown, 44,000 square feet, fully occupied
Precision Screw, 53,000 square feet, fully occupied with a CNC machine shop

Three major properties remain untouched, including:

Lincoln Mill, 3.5-acre property with 224,000-square-foot building with current renovation plans
Saco & Lowell Machine Shop, 3.5-acre property with 145,000-square-foot vacant building
Maine Energy Recovery Company, 8.45-acre city-owned property, currently vacant

THE SCHOOLS OF BIDDEFORD

John F. Kennedy Memorial School
Biddeford Primary School
Biddeford Intermediate School
Biddeford Middle School

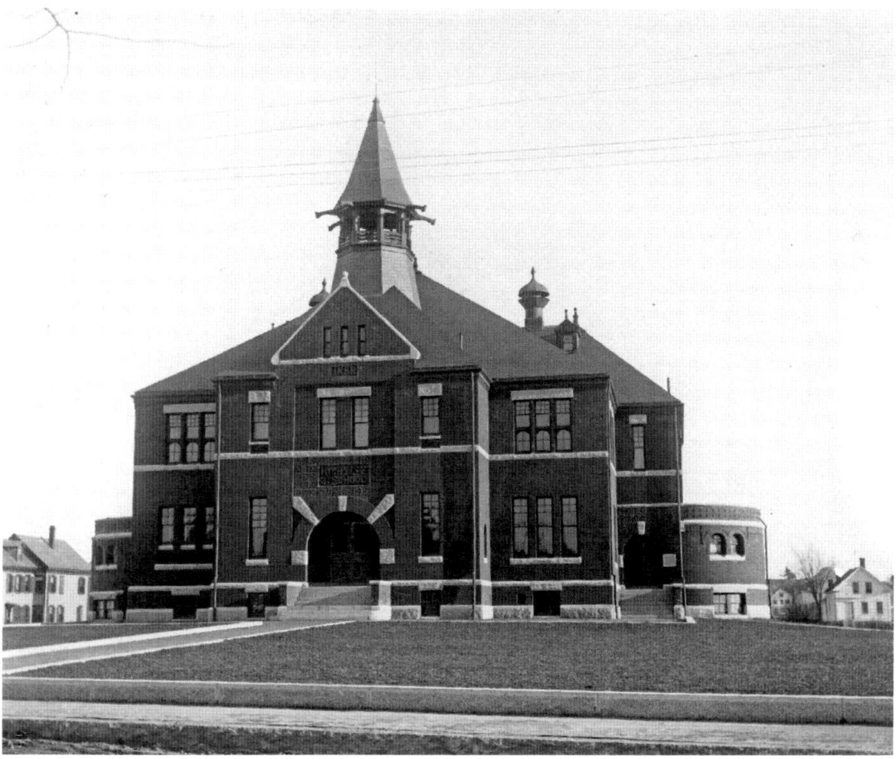

Biddeford High School, pictured on Alfred Street circa 1890, is now a recreational building for the community. *McArthur Public Library Archive.*

Biddeford Regional Center of Technology
Biddeford High School
St. James Catholic School
Heartwood College of Art
University of New England

THE CHURCHES OF BIDDEFORD

St. Joseph Church
St. Mary Church (closed 2009)
St. Andre Church (closed 2010)
St. Brendan Chapel
Union Church
GracePoint Church
New Life Christian Fellowship
Second Congregational Church

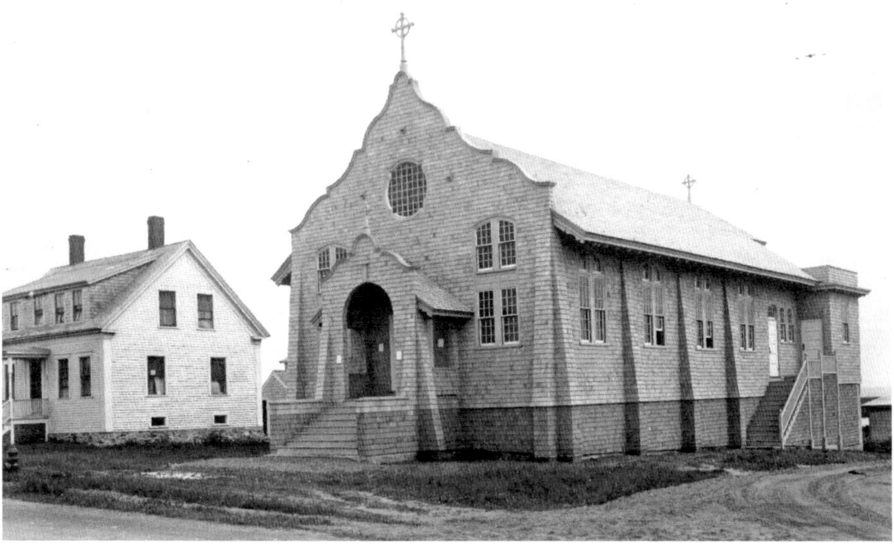

St. Brendan's Roman Catholic Church in Biddeford Pool, pictured here around 1916, continues to offer Catholic service on weekends during the summer for vacationers and local parishioners. *Robert H. Gay Photograph Collection, courtesy of McArthur Public Library.*

Notes

Chapter 1

1. Owen, *Old Times in Saco*, 2.
2. Ibid., 1.
3. Ibid., 2.
4. Fairfield, *Sands, Spindles, and Steeples*, 3.
5. Yorke, *History and Stories of Biddeford*, 7.
6. DesRoberts, "Biddeford History & Heritage Project."
7. Yorke, *History and Stories of Biddeford*, 7.
8. Bolton, *Real Founders of New England*, 24.
9. Ibid.
10. Folsom, *History of Saco and Biddeford*, 23.
11. Ibid.
12. Russell, *Indian New England*, 28.
13. Folsom, *History of Saco and Biddeford*, 23.

Chapter 2

14. Owen, *Old Times in Saco*, 6.
15. Ibid.

16. Yorke, *History and Stories of Biddeford*, 13.
17. Fairfield, *Sands, Spindles, and Steeples*, 4.
18. *Romance of the Pepperell*, 24.
19. Owen, *Old Times in Saco*, 12.
20. *Romance of the Pepperell*, 25.
21. Ibid.
22. Yorke, *History and Stories of Biddeford*, 15.
23. Owen, *Old Times in Saco*, 14.
24. Ibid., 17.

CHAPTER 3

25. Owen, *Old Times in Saco*, 57.
26. Churchill, Judd and Eastman, *Maine*, 70.
27. Ibid., 70.
28. Folsom, *History of Saco and Biddeford.*
29. Owen, *Old Times in Saco*, 19.
30. Churchill, Judd and Eastman, *Maine*, 57.
31. Owen, *Old Times in Saco*, 19.
32. Ibid.
33. Ibid., 22.
34. Churchill, Judd and Eastman, *Maine*, 58.
35. Folsom, *History of Saco and Biddeford.*
36. Ibid.
37. Owen, *Old Times in Saco*, 23-4.
38. Ibid., 29.
39. Ibid., 30-1.

CHAPTER 4

40. Bourne, *Red King's Rebellion*, 213.
41. Ibid.
42. Folsom, *History of Saco and Biddeford*, 153.
43. DesRoberts, "Biddeford History & Heritage Project."
44. Folsom, *History of Saco and Biddeford.*

45. Owen, *Old Times in Saco*, 36.
46. Ibid., 36–7.
47. Ibid., 41–2.
48. Yorke, *History and Stories of Biddeford*, 90.
49. Bourne, *Red King's Rebellion*, 241.
50. Ibid., 243.
51. Ibid., 242.
52. Yorke.

Chapter 5

53. *Romance of the Pepperell*, 9.
54. Ibid.
55. Ibid., 18.
56. Fairfield, *Sands, Spindles, and Steeples*, 13.
57. *Romance of the Pepperell,* 18.
58. Fairfield, *Sands, Spindles, and Steeples*, 17–18.
59. Churchill, Judd and Eastman, *Maine*, 69–70.
60. Yorke, *Men and Times*, 104.
61. Owen, *Old Times in Saco*, 54–5.
62. Fairfield, *Sands, Spindles, and Steeples*, 22–3.
63. Churchill, Judd and Eastman, *Maine*, 265.
64. Ibid.
65. Sprague, *Agreeable Situations,* 25.
66. Fairfield, *Sands, Spindles, and Steeples*, 23.
67. Churchill, Judd and Eastman, *Maine*, 147.

Chapter 6

68. Fairfield, *Sands, Spindles, and Steeples*, 18.
69. Ibid., 18.
70. Owen, *Old Times in Saco*, 69.
71. Fairfield, *Sands, Spindles, and Steeples*, 18–19.
72. Downs, *Pictorial History*, 29.
73. DesRoberts, "Biddeford History & Heritage Project."

74. Sprague, *Agreeable Situations*, 68.
75. Ibid., 104.
76. Fairfield, *Sands, Spindles, and Steeples*, 31.

CHAPTER 7

77. Fairfield, *Sands, Spindles, and Steeples*, 33.
78. Ibid., 45.
79. Ibid., 34.
80. Yorke, *Men and Times*, 11.
81. Ibid.
82. Sprague, *Agreeable Situations*, 31.
83. Yorke, *Men and Times*, 11–13.
84. *Romance of the Pepperell*, 6.
85. Yorke, *Men and Times*, 14.
86. Ibid., 21.

CHAPTER 8

87. Fairfield, *Sands, Spindles, and Steeples*, 51.
88. Ibid., 52.
89. *Maine Granite Quarries and Prospects*.
90. Fairfield, *Sands, Spindles, and Steeples*, 47.
91. Yorke, *Men and Times*, 16.
92. Fairfield, *Sands, Spindles, and Steeples*, 46.
93. Moran, *Belles of New England*, 33.
94. Fairfield, *Sands, Spindles, and Steeples*, 47.
95. Knowlton, *Pepperell Progress*.

CHAPTER 9

96. Yorke, *Men and Times*, 27.
97. Ibid., 30.

98. Ibid., 32.
99. Ibid., 36.
100. Ibid., 38.
101. Ibid.
102. Ibid., 42.

CHAPTER 10

103. Shevenell, *Home Road*, online.
104. Guignard, *La Foi—La Langue—La Culture.*
105. *Union and Journal*, January 3, 1862.
106. Guignard, 115, 120.
107. *Union and Journal*, January 3, 1862.
108. Ibid., June 6, 1862.
109. Ibid., January 3, 1862.
110. *Maine Democrat*, April 18, 1865.
111. *Union and Journal*, various editions.

CHAPTER 11

112. Guignard, *La Foi—La Langue—La Culture*, 19–20.
113. Ibid.
114. Ibid., 92.
115. Ibid., 93.
116. Ibid.
117. Ibid.

CHAPTER 12

118. *Maine Democrat*, January 4, 1853.
119. Ibid., January 18, 1853.
120. Ibid., January 25, 1853.
121. Ibid., November 10, 1863.
122. Ibid.

CHAPTER 13

123. DesRoberts, "Biddeford History & Heritage Project."
124. Yorke, *History and Stories of Biddeford*, 61.
125. Ibid., 60.
126. Smith, *Gleanings*, 21.
127. *Weekly Record*, July 28, 1910.
128. Ibid.
129. United States census data.

CHAPTER 14

130. Yorke, *History and Stories of Biddeford*, 65.
131. *Weekly Record*, March, 25, 1915.
132. *Biddeford Daily Journal*, January 6, 1917.
133. Yorke, *History and Stories of Biddeford*, 65.
134. *Biddeford Daily Journal*, February 6, 1917.
135. Yorke, *History and Stories of Biddeford*, 65.
136. Ibid.
137. *Biddeford Daily Journal*, March 26, 1917.
138. Kanes, "Uncomfortable History."
139. Ibid.
140. DesRoberts, "Biddeford History & Heritage Project."

CHAPTER 15

141. *Biddeford Daily Journal*, December 13, 1941.
142. Ibid., September 2, 1943.
143. Ibid., September 7, 1943.
144. Bouthillette, personal letters.
145. *Biddeford Daily Journal*, advertisements.
146. Ibid., September 3, 1943.

CHAPTER 16

147. "Burning of the Hooper Street Tenements."
148. *Journal Tribune*, October 31, 2007.
149. Ibid.
150. Ibid.
151. *Journal Tribune*, May 13, 2006.
152. Annual Report: 1956.
153. Annual Report: 1958.
154. Ibid.
155. DesRoberts, "Biddeford History & Heritage Project."

CHAPTER 17

156. Garson, "Outsourcing," 229.
157. Ibid., 231–32.
158. Mehlsak, "Biddeford Firm Has the Competition Covered."
159. Ibid.
160. Garson, "Outsourcing," 239.
161. Nordheimer, "Downsized, but Not Out," 12.
162. Ibid.
163. Ibid.
164. Ibid.

CHAPTER 18

165. Graham, "Rebuilding La Kermesse."
166. Bouchard, "MERC," 1B.
167. Burnett, "MERC," 3.
168. Bouchard, "MERC," 1B.
169. Bartlett, "Incinerator Test Scheduled in Fall," 3.
170. Ibid.
171. Bouchard, "MERC," 1B.
172. Ibid.
173. Perkins, "Letter to the Editor," 13.

174. Mehlsak, "MERC Troubles May Lead to Walkout," A1–3.
175. Ibid.
176. Zaitlin, quoted in *Portland Press Herald*, April 27, 1989, 38.
177. Burnett, "MERC," 3.
178. Ibid.

Chapter 19

179. Bouchard, "MERC," 1B.
180. Ibid.
181. Wright, "Two Biddefords."
182. Ibid.
183. Ibid.
184. Annual Report: 1954.

Chapter 20

185. Seaver, "Top-25."
186. "Nutting Tours Downtown."
187. Ibid.
188. Seaver, "Top-25."
189. Downtown Development Commission, June 30, 2004.
190. Ibid.
191. Bodwell, "Mayor of the Mill."
192. Baumer, "Biddeford's Mills at Center of Downtown Revival."
193. Ibid.
194. Graham, "Redevelopment of Pepperell Mill Complex Boosts Biddeford's Image."

Chapter 21

195. Farwell, "Where Possibilities Loom."
196. Ibid.

197. Ibid.
198. *Biddeford Mill District Master Plan*, 2009.
199. Wright, "Two Biddefords."
200. Ibid.
201. "Heart & Soul: Reinventing a Mill City's Downtown," online.
202. Ibid.
203. Ibid.

Chapter 22

204. Wright, "Two Biddefords."
205. Hench, "Residents Ask Relief."
206. Ibid.
207. Graham, "Biddeford Serving as Incubator for Business."
208. Ibid., "Biddeford Without MERC."
209. Ibid., "Biddeford Serving as Incubator for Business."
210. Ibid.
211. Ibid., "Biddeford Sheds 'Trashtown' Image."
212. Ibid.
213. Graham, "Biddeford Ready to Redevelop Former MERC Property."
214. Ibid.

Chapter 23

215. Graham, "Biddeford Sheds 'Trashtown' Image."
216. Baumer, "Biddeford's Mills at Center of Downtown Revival."
217. Graham, "Biddeford Serving as Incubator for Business."
218. Ibid.
219. Goad, "Biscuit Baker Rises to Occasion."
220. Graham, "Biddeford Sheds 'Trashtown' Image."
221. Ibid., "Downtown Biddeford's All Abuzz."

Chapter 24

222. Graham, "Redevelopment of Pepperell Mill."
223. Ibid.
224. "How the Mill Impacts Biddeford," *Pepperell Mill Campus*.
225. Graham, "Downtown Biddeford's All Abuzz."
226. Baumer, "Biddeford's Mills at Center of Downtown Revival."

Chapter 25

227. Graham, "Biddeford Sheds 'Trashtown' Image."
228. Ibid.
229. Annual Report: 1954.
230. Graham, "Downtown Biddeford's All Abuzz."
231. Bennett, "City Sidewalks Create Uncertainty."
232. Ibid.
233. Graham, "Businesses Uprooted by Progress."
234. Ibid.
235. Ibid.

Chapter 26

236. Aloisio, "Biddeford's Roots Begin with 'Vines'."
237. Graham, "Downtown Biddeford's All Abuzz"
238. United States census data, 2015.
239. Graham, "Downtown Biddeford's All Abuzz"
240. Beaupre, *Interview*.
241. Ibid.

Sources

Aloisio, Anthony. "Biddeford's Roots Begin with 'Vines'." *Biddeford-Saco-OOB Courier*, October 10, 2016.

Bartlett, Joel. "Incinerator Test Scheduled in Fall." *Journal Tribune*, July 24, 1986.

Baumer, Jim. "Biddeford's Mills at Center of Downtown Revival." *Boston Globe*, February 8, 2015.

Beaupré, Norman. "The Corner Grocery Stores of My Youth." *Biddeford-Saco-OOB Courier*, July 14, 2016.

———. *Interview*. October 8, 2016.

———. "The Potpourri." *Biddeford-Saco-OOB Courier*, December 17, 2015.

———. "St. Francis College and my memories." *Biddeford-Saco-OOB Courier*, July 30, 2015.

Bennett, Alan. "City Sidewalks Create Uncertainty in Biddeford." *Journal Tribune*, October 15, 2016.

Biddeford Daily Journal. "Deplorable Conditions at City Homestead: Shocking Beyond Belief of Newsmen." January 4, 1956.

Biddeford Daily Journal, 1917–43.

"Biddeford Mayors: Since 1855, the Year of the City Charter." McArthur Public Library. http://www.mcarthurpubliclibrary.org/biddeford-mayors.html.

Biddeford Mill District Master Plan. City of Biddeford. 2009. http://www.biddefordmaine.org.

Biddeford-Saco-OOB Courier. "Lincoln Mill Building Up for Auction." March 24, 1994: 2.

———. "Nutting Tours Downtown, Encourages Optimism." November 24, 2003.

Biddeford Weekly Journal, 1901–05.

Bodwell, Joshua. "The Mayor of the Mill." *Maine Home + Design*. March 2009.

Bolton, Charles K. *The Real Founders of New England*. Boston: F.W. Faxon, 1929.

Bouchard, Kelley. "MERC: A Point of Reckoning for 'Trash Town U.S.A.'" *Portland Press Herald*, February 27, 2000.

Bourne, Russell. *The Red King's Rebellion*. New York: Athenewm, 1990.

Bouthillette, Roland. Personal letters and journal. In the author's possession. 1944–45.

Brayley, Arthur W. *History of the Granite Industry of New England*. Boston: E.L. Grimes Company, 1913.

Burnett, Lee. "MERC: How Did It Ever Get There?" *Journal Tribune*, October 21, 1989, A1 & A3.

"Burning of the Hooper Street Tenements, Biddeford, 1963." Maine Memory Network. April 20, 1963. https://www.mainememory.net.

Churchill, Edwin A., Richard Judd and Joel Eastman. *Maine: The Pine Tree State from Prehistory to the Present*. Orono: University of Maine Press, 1995.

City of Biddeford. Annual Report: 1954. McArthur Public Library Archive.

———. Annual Report: 1955. McArthur Public Library Archive.

———. Annual Report: 1957. McArthur Public Library Archive.

———. Annual Report: 1958. McArthur Public Library Archive.

———. Annual Report: 1961. McArthur Public Library Archive.

———. Annual Report: 1967. McArthur Public Library Archive.

———. Annual Report: 1969. McArthur Public Library Archive.

———. Annual Report: 1970–71. McArthur Public Library Archive.

———. Annual Report: 1976. McArthur Public Library Archive.

Davis, William A. "Long Hesitant, Biddeford Embraces Renewal." *Boston Globe*, November 4, 2007.

DesRoberts, Renee. "Biddeford History & Heritage Project." Maine Memory Network. https://www.mainememory.net.

Downs, Jacques. *A Pictorial History: The Cities on the Saco*. Norfolk, VA: Donning Company, 1985.

Downtown Development Commission Meeting Minutes. *City of Biddeford*. June 30, 2004.

Fairfield, Roy P. *Sands, Spindles, and Steeples*. Portland, ME: House of Falmouth, 1956.

Farwell, Jackie. "Where Possibilities Loom: Biddeford Marks the End of Its Textile Era, with One Foot Firmly in the Future." MaineBiz, June 15, 2009. http://www.mainebiz.biz.

"Fire Inside of Diamond National Lumberyard, Biddeford, 1963." Maine Memory Network. April 20, 1963. https://www.mainememory.net.

Folsom, George. *History of Saco and Biddeford*. Saco, ME: Alex C. Putnam, 1830.

Garson, Barbara. "Outsourcing." In *Money Makes the World Go Around*. New York: Viking, 2001.

Goad, Meredith. "Biscuit Baker Rises to Occasion, Wins Biddeford Startup Funds." *Portland Press Herald*, January 22, 2014.

———. "Plans for Biddeford's Lincoln Mill Changed to Double Number of Market-Rate Apartments." *Portland Press Herald*, February 25, 2016.

Graham, Gillian. "Biddeford Announces Encore Main Street Challenge." *Press Herald*, October 8, 2013.

———. "Biddeford Planning Board Approves Changes to Lincoln Mill Project." *Portland Press Herald*, March 3, 2016.

———. "Biddeford Ready to Redevelop Former MERC Property." *Portland Press Herald*, July 15, 2015.

———. "Biddeford Serving as Incubator for Businesses in Their Infancy." *Portland Press Herald*, November 19, 2012.

———. "Biddeford Sheds 'Trashtown' Image as Developers Invest in Historic Mill Buildings." *Portland Press Herald*, August 10, 2015.

———. "Biddeford Without MERC: 'We Will No Longer Be Known as a Stink Town'." *Portland Press Herald*, November 30, 2012.

———. "Businesses Uprooted by Progress at Biddeford's Lincoln Mill." *Portland Press Herald*, February 23, 2015.

———. "Developer Plans to Buy WestPoint Mill." *Biddeford-Saco-OOB Courier*, May 27, 2010.

———. "Downtown Biddeford's All Abuzz, but the Parking's a Buzzkill." *Portland Press Herald*, November 30, 2016.

———. "MERC Closing Incinerator in Biddeford." *Portland Press Herald*, November 1, 2012.

———. "Rebuilding La Kermesse." *Portland Press Herald*, June 18, 2012.

———. "Redevelopment of Pepperell Mill Complex Boosts Biddeford's Image." *Portland Press Herald*, August 16, 2014.

Guignard, Michael J. *La Foi—La Langue—La Culture: The Franco-Americans of Biddeford, Maine*. Self-published, 1984.

"Heart & Soul: Reinventing a Mill City's Downtown." The Orton Family Foundation. October 23, 2012. http://www.orton.org.

Hench, David. "Residents Ask Relief from Smell of MERC." *Portland Press Herald*, June 24, 2011.

Journal Tribune. "Pepperell Manufacturing to WestPoint Home." May 13, 2006: C7.

———. "Remembering the Great Fire of 1947." Special edition. October 31, 2007.

Kanes, Candace. "Uncomfortable History." *Maine History Online*. Maine Historical Society, undated.

Killelea, Elaine Frederick. "The Week that Maine Burned." *Portland Press Herald*, October 7, 2012.

Knowlton, Evelyn H. *Pepperell Progress*. Cambridge, MA: Harvard University Press, 1948.

Littlefield, Lizzie. Personal diary. McArthur Public Library Archive. 1888–94.

Maine Democrat, 1865–75.

Maine Granite Quarries and Prospects: Report of Maine Geological Survey. Augusta, ME: 1958.

Marcil, Fr. George. *Franciscans in Biddeford, Maine 1933–1975*. December 1976.

Mason, Ella Jordan. *History, Old High School Biddeford, Maine*. 1848–81.

Mehlsak, Mo. "Biddeford Firm Has the Competition Covered." *Journal Tribune*, September 28, 1988.

Mehlsak, Mo, and Lee Burnett. "MERC Troubles May Lead to Walkout." *Journal Tribune*, August 18, 1988.

Mendros, Dina. "A Final Farewell to the Mill Era." *Journal Tribune*, August 8, 2009, A1–3.

Moran, William. *The Belles of New England: The Women of the Textile Mills and the Families Whose Wealth They Wove*. New York: St. Martin's Press, 2002.

Murphy, Edward D. "Deal Reached to Shutter MERC Plant." *Portland Press Herald*, June 29, 2012.

———. "MERC Task Force Reports Progress." *Portland Press Herald*, August 20, 2009, 1B.

Murphy, Grace. "MERC Trash Odor Plan to Cost Over $1 Million." *Portland Press Herald*, December 17, 1999: 2B.

Muszynski, Kristen. "A Time for Franco Pride." *Journal Tribune*, June 28–29, 2008.

National Main Street Center, Inc. Accessed December 4, 2016. http://www.mainstreet.org.

New England Historical Society. "The Year a State Burned: Maine Fires of 1947." October 9, 2015.

Nordheimer, Jon. "Downsized, but Not Out: A Mill Town's Tale." *New York Times*, March 9, 1997.

O'Connell, Kathleen. "Local Textile Workers End Strike." *Biddeford-Saco Journal*, April 20, 1976: 2.

———. "Textile Companies Put On Notice." *Biddeford-Saco Journal*, February 10, 1976, 12.

Owen, Daniel E. *Old Times in Saco*. Saco, ME: Biddeford Times Press, 1891.

Pepperell Mill Campus Newsletter. "How the Mill Impacts Biddeford." October 20, 2016.

Perkins, Dana. "Letter to the Editor." *Journal Tribune*, August 25, 1988, 13.

The Romance of the Pepperell. Boston: Walton Advertising and Printing, 1921.

Russell, Howard S. *Indian New England Before the Mayflower*. Hanover, NH: University Press of New England, 1980.

Schaub, Robert H. "Fortunes Rocks: Some of Its History." *Biddeford Weekly Journal*, August 31, 1928.

Schwartz, Brett. "Youth with a Voice: Biddeford, ME." *National Association of Development Organizations*. April 29, 2013. https://www.nado.org.

Seaver, Randy. "The Top-25 Biddeford-Saco Political Players and Coaches." *Randy Seaver Consulting*, January 18, 2012. https://randyseaver.com.

Smith, Joseph. *Gleanings from the Sea: Showing the Pleasures, Pains and Penalties of Life Afloat with Contingencies Ashore.* Minnesota: Chas C. Whitney, 1887.

Sneddon, Rob. "A Battle Lost." *DownEast*, October 13, 2015. http://downeast.com/football-battle-lost.

Sprague, Laura Fecych. *Agreeable Situations: Society, Commerce, and Art in Southern Maine 1780–1830*. Kennebunk, ME: The Brick Store Museum, 1987.

Union and Journal, 1853–75.

Weekly Record, 1910–15.

Wright, Virginia. "The Two Biddefords." *DownEast*, June 2007. http://downeast.com/june-2007.

Yorke, Dane. *A History and Stories of Biddeford.* Biddeford, ME: McArthur Public Library, 1994.

———. *The Men and Times of Pepperell: An Account of the First One Hundred Years of the Pepperell Manufacturing Company, Incorporated February 16, 1844*. Boston: Pepperell Manufacturing Company, 1945.

INDEX

About the Author

The history of French Canadians coming to Biddeford, Maine, is played out in the ancestry of our author, Emma Bouthillette. She is a fourth-generation Franco-American, with Canadian heritage stemming from both sides of her family.

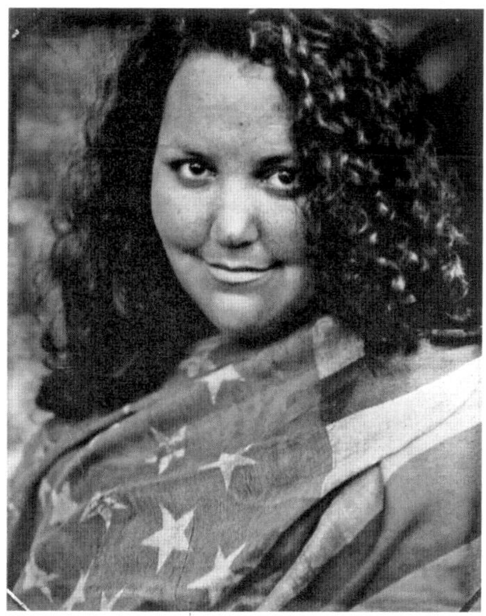

Courtesy of Kari Wehrs.

Born in Biddeford, Bouthillette actually spent her first five years across the river in Saco before her parents built their home on Pool Road in Biddeford. Growing up, her father told her the cubby in the closet was to hide from the Sokoki who still roamed the woods surrounding their house. He scared her by telling her tales of native tribes baiting Englishmen—folklore that was born of the French and Indian Wars that ravaged the area some three hundred years earlier.

After school and on summer vacations, Bouthillette's grandparents spoiled her during endless hours at their beachfront homes. With Pépère Croteau and Pépère Roland (her maternal and paternal grandfathers), she learned to count by playing cribbage. With her Mémère Croteau and Mémère B (her maternal grandmother and great-grandmother), she learned to knit and enjoy the time-honored traditions of cooking for the family. When in her grandparents' care, Bouthillette loved to listen to their stories of days gone by. Pépère Roland would tell her about how he met and courted her Mémère Gisele. Mémère Croteau would talk about buying a new pair of shoes at Butlers just to go out dancing on the Pier in Old Orchard Beach. Pépère Croteau would tell her about the butcher shop where he used to cut meat, and all the other little corner stores that filled Biddeford's downtown. She dreamed of their life in Biddeford, which was a far cry from the abandoned storefronts and forgotten mill buildings.

There was nothing in Biddeford, and by the time she graduated Biddeford High School, she had grand plans to move "away." However, through a series of events, she ended up enrolling at the University of New England and commuted from her parents' home, just a mile down the road. During her sophomore year, she petitioned to attend a senior-level class taught by Dr. Elizabeth A. DeWolfe. It was the first time in all her academic career that Bouthillette found history even remotely intriguing. While pursuing a bachelor's in fine arts in English literature, Bouthillette took enough courses with DeWolfe to declare a minor in history. She was given the opportunity, along with her classmate Camille Smalley, to research the history of mill girls with a focus on Biddeford's textile industry. She suddenly began to see those looming brick mill buildings as something more than vacant and downtrodden.

Since graduating college in 2008, Bouthillette has written for the *Kennebunk Post*, *Biddeford-Saco-OOB Courier*, the *Portland Press Herald*, *Journal Tribune*, *Maine Women's Magazine* and *UNE Alumni Magazine*. She further pursued her passion for writing by attending University of Southern Maine's Stonecoast and earning her master's in creative nonfiction writing. Much of her work has focused on Biddeford and her desire to tell the stories of her fellow neighbors and a city being reborn. Bouthillette also became involved in the city's revitalization through volunteer work with Heart of Biddeford and Engine.

Bouthillette continues to freelance write for various publications, but has shifted her career to the legal field as an assistant at Norman, Hanson

& DeTroy, LLC. When not at work or writing, you can probably find Bouthillette enjoying Fortunes Rocks Beach with Savvy, her Pembroke Welsh Corgi, or at one of Biddeford's fine downtown establishments enjoying the vibrant community in which she lives.